Battleground Europe

SOMME
FRICOURT-MAMETZ

Battleground Europe
SOMME
FRICOURT-MAMETZ

Michael Stedman

Series editor
Nigel Cave

LEO COOPER
London

First published in 1997 by
LEO COOPER
an imprint of
Pen & Sword Books Limited
47 Church Street, Barnsley, South Yorkshire S70 2AS

ISBN 0 85052 574 8

A CIP catalogue of this book is available
from the British Library

Printed by Redwood Books Limited
Trowbridge, Wiltshire

*For up-to-date information on other titles produced under
the Leo Cooper imprint, please telephone or write to:*

Pen & Sword Books Ltd, FREEPOST, 47 Church Street
Barnsley, South Yorkshire S70 2AS
Telephone 01226 734222

CONTENTS

Introduction by Series Editor

This is the fifth book in the Battleground Europe series to cover a part of the Front Line that existed on 1st July 1916 on the British sector of the battlefield of the Somme. The number of books on this sparsely populated, rather unexciting part of northern France and, indeed, the market for them, is a sign of how firmly etched on the national consciousness are the events of that day. The debate about its military significance – even in the medium term – will doubtless rumble on for years to come; but many Britons who come out here to visit are following the steps of an ancestor or of a community. They are often not interested in the concerns of the generals but rather of the experience of the junior officer, soldier or, at the most, of a battalion on *Der Tag,* and, occasionally, what happened over the subsequent weeks and months over this pleasant, rolling chalk land.

Michael Stedman, in the third of his books in this series on the Somme, writes with fervour and feeling about what took place here at Fricourt and in the smaller neighbouring village of Mametz in the days leading up to the great day and immediately subsequently. He explains the problems that faced the planners of the British offensive created by Fricourt's jutting position in the German line as it turned in an easterly direction from this pivot point. The action, the disasters and the successes are all closely related to the ground, which is the hall mark of the series.

The book also concerns itself with the personalities that have become well established with the literary public – Siegfried Sassoon, Robert Graves and the lesser known, but most powerful and moving author, Bernard Adams. A large number make the pilgrimage to the grave of the young poet, Noel Hodgson, at Mansell Copse; now it is possible to follow what happened to him and other members of his battalion on that fateful sunny morning in July.

The front is put in the context of the rest of the military machine that was required to support them – the railways, the dumps and the Casualty Clearing Stations. It is not unusual for the work of those behind the horrors of the front to get lost. In this respect the book tries to set the balance by pointing out what remains of the traces of the massive investment in men, material and machinery that was poured into this hitherto rather sleepy part of France.

The book touches on the events of March and August 1918; all too often British generalship is examined and judged on a single day's activity in a war that lasted for well over four years. These men, and those who served them, deserve a rather more broad ranging and open minded critical examination. Too frequently we are told how the Germans swept away the hard won gains of the 1916 Somme offensive in a matter of days; contrarily, we are told all too little about the epic achievements of the British Army in the Hundred Days of 1918, from 8 August to the Armistice on 11 November.

The countryside around Fricourt and behind the old line towards the Somme is relatively undisturbed by the rush of the modern world. In this pleasant and tranquil location there are numerous eloquent reminders of the ferocity of the fighting that took place so many decades ago, not least the shattered ground from the massive mines or the beautiful solitude within the boundaries of the large number of British war cemeteries. What happened around here is only a small part of the vast conflict that enveloped Europe between 1914 and 1918; but a sound understanding of this should lead to a greater willingness to know more about what it was that drove men to such great displays of sacrifice. There is nothing more disheartening to read in the visitors' registers such comments as, Why and For what did they die?. Surely it is our responsibility to seek these answers, and I firmly hope that books such as those in this series will help to encourage later generations not only to admire but to understand those who fought and suffered and, in many cases, died here. The book is designed to satisfy the interest of those who visit Fricourt and Mametz, curious about their parts in the much greater Somme battle; it is for the visitor to seek from other sources explanations of why there was a battle and indeed why the war was fought at all.

Nigel Cave.
Ely Place, London.

Author's introduction

As at La Boisselle to the north, the fighting at Fricourt and Mametz was frequently punctured by the detonation of mines, occasionally massive and sometimes of lesser significance. These have left many visible scars and the sites of Bois Francais and the Triple Tambour are well known to visitors as places where the impact of these vast explosions are still visible, eight decades on. But even more apparent to the casual visitor here are the cemeteries; so many that it almost defies belief that such enormous numbers of men were killed during the fighting for this relatively small tract of territory. Due south of the village, in the direction of Bray-sur-Somme, a whole string of Commonwealth War Graves Commission cemeteries dominate the land. In Bray there is also a French National Cemetery, testimony to the many Frenchmen who were killed on the Somme during 1914-15. Incidentally, Bray-sur-Somme was home to a number of base hospitals as well as many supply and command facilities which are of relevance to the Fricourt area. Immediately to the north of Fricourt, on the road leading towards Contalmaison, is one of the few German cemeteries to be found on the Somme. It is enormous, brooding, almost menacing in atmosphere. Within the village of Fricourt and west towards Becordel-Becourt are a series of interesting and distinctive British cemeteries, containing many graves of the casualties incurred in late June and throughout the fighting here in the summer of 1916. Further west along that road, the D938 towards Albert, is the massive French National Cemetery into which most of the graves belonging to Frenchmen killed fighting in this area, north of the Somme, during the first two years of the war were concentrated. West and south-west of Albert are the villages of Dernancourt, Morlancourt and Buire-sur-l'Ancre which are also covered by this guide and where many men killed during the Second Battle of Albert and other fighting during 1918 are buried.

However, it is not just the cemeteries and craters which attract so many visitors. The area's subtle atmosphere, the intricacy of the trench lines and the constant evolution of the tactical balance throughout 1915 – 16 and 1918 captures so many people's interest. Without an adequate understanding of the topography of the battlefield and a handy map and guide it is easy to lose one's way here amongst the areas many valleys and intersecting spurs. The area is both intimate and yet attractive, retaining a huge number of evocative and poignant links with contemporary literature and poetry. No history or guide dealing with the terrible events which occurred here can afford to ignore the words of the poets and chroniclers of the war. In attempting to sense the atmosphere of the battle here I have quoted a passage of words from Sassoon's book, *'Memoirs of an Infantry Officer.'* They were written to describe the scene as he waited in the darkness, high on the hillsides above Dernancourt, for the return of his battalion. They seem to me to be a timeless and evocative recreation of the atmosphere after battle has subsided.

'Now there came an interval of silence in which I heard a horse neigh, shrill and scared and lonely. Then the procession of the returning troops began. The camp-fires were burning low when the grinding jolting column lumbered back. The field guns came first, with nodding men sitting stiffly on weary horses, followed by waggons and limbers and field-kitchens. After this rumble of wheels came the infantry, shambling, limping, straggling and out of step. If anyone spoke it was only a muttered word, and the mounted officers rode as if asleep. The men had carried their emergency water in petrol-cans, against which bayonets made a hollow clink; except for the shuffling of feet, this was the only sound. Thus, with an almost spectral appearance, the lurching brown figures flitted past with slung rifles and heads bent forward under basin-helmets.'

Limping. Shuffling. Spectral. Bent. Words carefully chosen by Sassoon to remove any sense of vanity or glory from the scene he revealed, exposing the suffering endured by the hundreds of thousands who passed in similar empty silence through these tiny villages. A visit here truly provides an opportunity to contemplate the awfulness of war.

Yet today Fricourt is a fine place to visit. But, unlike Thiepval or La Boisselle, it is not the popular first port of call for many parties and inexperienced students. Fricourt can therefore be visited at your leisure, in order to allow the wonderful panoramas which it affords across much of the British sector of the Somme battlefield to reveal themselves. In the history of the first day of the Battle of the Somme, 1st July 1916, the village of Fricourt is unique in that it was not the subject of frontal attack at 7.30 am that fateful morning. Elsewhere it is possible to visualise an almost continuous attempt, by thousands of British troops, to advance across No Man's Land at the onset of those momentous events. But here at Fricourt the story unfolded quite differently. The fundamental cause was that Fricourt lay at an apex in the British front line. From Serre southwards the British lines ran in an almost unbroken southerly direction until reaching Fricourt, at which point they turned eastwards, heading off towards Mametz and beyond.

Fricourt village was therefore a most significant German salient. There are two locations close to Fricourt which give access to these splendid views. The first vantage point lies on the northern boundary of this guide, and looks across from the vicinity of the Willow Patch and Scots Redoubt towards La Boisselle and the Tara – Usna lines. The second lies to the east of the Bois Francais, the present day Bois d' Engremont on your IGN map, in the fields above Mansell Copse. From these heights, south of Mametz, you can see almost all of the southern end of the British sector including Carnoy and the village of Maricourt where the British and French armies abutted at the outset of the battle and the locations which were expected to be taken, Fricourt, Mametz and Montauban in the distance.

In this context Fricourt is a splendid location at which to learn about and understand the Battle of the Somme. The proximity of large French and German cemeteries gives the study of this area a balance and perspective for school students which the stories of some other locations lack. The German cemetery at Fricourt is powerful and evocative and can make a great impression upon the young. All I would counsel is that this place cannot be hurried. To skimp Fricourt is like doing the Louvre in Paris in one hour. To trivialise by rushing will simply undermine what could be learned. You cannot appreciate the new understanding of something when you are enslaved to an impossible timetable, and the Somme battlefield is no exception. Much better to set realistic targets for your visit and manage the time you can have here sensibly. Get to know this magnificent location of Fricourt in depth. Let careful observation and thoughtful questioning reveal all of the many layers of fact, insight and interpretation to yourself, your school party or your family and friends.

Of course, Fricourt and Mametz witness thousands of passing motorists every day. Amongst them many British vehicles pass speedily by the sites of these two villages, heading along the D938 in the direction of Peronne. But the complexity of the Fricourt story soon draws many experienced and knowledgeable people into the folds of its numerous valleys, spurs and woodlands. The reason is straightforward. Understanding here is not gained lightly. From within the village it is almost impossible to visualise a 'front line,' a No Man's Land or even from where the Tommies were coming! And the capture of Fricourt required imaginative preparation. Although the occupation of the village was undertaken within two days, the methods employed were innovative and are therefore interesting in the context of other attacks this day whose planning and execution lacked creativity or flair. And all this carried out by troops who were the very epitome of Kitchener's New Army, men whom Rawlinson, as Fourth Army commander, felt unable to trust, elsewhere, to undertake anything other than a clinically structured and somewhat mechanical advance.

Apart from Fricourt and Mametz this guide deals with the fighting which took place, north of Mametz village, for the approaches to Mametz Wood. The guide also pays special attention to the terrain south of Fricourt, going as far as Bray-sur-Somme. This leads into a discussion of the impact which the Battle of the Somme had on the areas which supplied the logistical support for the British Army here, especially the railheads at Dernancourt and its surrounding terrain. Because these villages, along with Albert, were the scene of much fighting during 1918 proper consideration is also given to the fighting during that year in those areas.

Michael Stedman.
Leigh, Worcester.

Acknowledgements

Within the narrative record of events here at Fricourt I have made considerable use of those many words, often penned in haste amidst terrible danger more than eighty years ago. To all of those soldiers who wrote at that time and those who penned their memoirs during the post war era I am grateful and can only stand in awe. However, it would have been impossible to complete this guide without the help of many of my contemporaries. In particular I should like to thank Nigel Cave who as always has undertaken a thorough review of this work and for whose sensible guidance and help I am very grateful; Jerry Gee and Derek Butler and other staff of the Commonwealth War Graves Commission at Maidenhead, Peter Hart, Mike Nicholson, Katie Doar and Phil Nash of Waterstones' Booksellers whose excellent specialised maps department, at 17 St. Ann's Square, Manchester, supplied my maps and through whom the requisite present day IGN maps of France can be obtained; Andre Belle of Fricourt, Bob Grundy, Charles Hambi, Major Tony Swift, Geoff Thomas and Derek Stevenson. Geoff and Derek have walked many miles of the Somme battlefield in all sorts of weather with me, but in their company the sun has always seemed to shine kindly. The staff at the Public Records Office in Kew have provided me with much help, assistance and considered judgement. Many members of the Western Front Association have also helped in greatly enhancing my knowledge of the Fricourt area. To all of these people I should like to extend my sincere thanks whilst making clear that any errors which remain within the text are solely of my own making.

Sensible equipment and advice for visitors

One of the greatest pleasures, and the most salutary and moving of experiences, is to "walk the course" of an event in the extraordinary history of the Great War, reconstructing in our minds the encounters of the men who were there and sharing the chance insights and discoveries with friends. I cannot forget the first time I saw and walked many of these places, the Salford Pals' attack on Thiepval on 1st July 1916, the tragic advance of the Tyneside battalions of the 34th Division at La Boisselle that same day, many of the Manchester Pals at Trones Wood west of Guillemont. But whoever you are following, or whatever you are trying to explain and understand, certain items are always likely to enhance your pleasure. It is worth noting that here in the Fricourt – Mametz district there are numerous small woodlands, especially east of the German front line positions, providing relief from the weather. The immediate area surrounding these two villages is compact and the walks I have described there should never take more than three hours. However, south of the Albert – Peronne road there are vast areas of exposed and open upland to walk. Here sun cream and plenty of drinks are absolutely essential, especially in hot summer weather. Stout shoes or walking boots at any time of the year are vital. Wellington boots and thick socks in winter or soon after rain are needed, along with appropriate outer clothing. Incidentally, you could attempt to complete the walks in the immediate vicinity of Fricourt and Mametz in one day. Therefore, for those of you intent on spending just such a full day here 'in the field' and who want to record your visit carefully some further items are advisable. Take a sandwich, a camera, a pen and notebook to record where you took your photographs and perhaps to note your visit in the cemetery registers. For those of you who choose to walk south of the Albert – Peronne road, up towards the Bois Francais, Point 110 areas and beyond I suggest a pair of binoculars will greatly enhance your understanding. Finally, take a decent penknife with a corkscrew, a first aid kit and a small rucksack capable of carrying everything comfortably.

Here at Fricourt, as at Thiepval, a metal detector is, let us be frank, an embarrassment. To be seen digging within sight of what should be a place of tranquillity and reflection is almost to desecrate the memory of those whose names are recorded so starkly on the Memorial to the Missing which dominates the skyline to the north of the Albert to Bapaume road. The spectacle of lone Britons sweeping their electronic plates across empty fields fills me with sadness. This is a place where a more rewarding and meaningful history reveals itself, without recourse to indignity.

No significant preparation is required to cope with medical requirements. It is however very sensible to ensure that you carry an E111 form which gives reciprocal rights to medical and hospital treatment in France, as well as all other EC countries. The necessary documents can be obtained free from any main post office. As in the UK where you are in a working agricultural area and may be scratched or cut by rusty metals, ensure that your tetanus vaccination is up to date. Comprehensive personal and vehicle insurance is advisable, at the very least Green Card insurance (often available free from your vehicle insurers) is a legal requirement when motoring abroad. In this context it is worth noting that there have been an increasing number of thefts from British tourists' vehicles in the area of the Somme, even when parked near to the many cemeteries and features around Fricourt. To help arrange and plan your stay I have identified a list of campsites, hotels and B&B accommodation within easy distance of Fricourt in Chapter 1, which deals with the designated area today. However, a fuller guide to the many excellent hotels, restaurants, auberges and overnight accommodations available in the Picardie area can be obtained from the Comite Regional du Tourisme de Picardie, 3 Rue Vincent Auriol – 80000 Amiens – Tel: 00 33 322 91 10 15.

How to use this book

This guide can be used in preparation for your visit, in front of the fire at home on a cold winter evening. In that case it is perhaps best read from start to finish. I think you will have a sound feel for Fricourt at the end of one or two evenings' reading and might be ready to book your cross channel ferry or tunnel for those days in March and April when the weather begins to clear, the fields are ploughed and crop growth has not yet hidden the detail and topography of the ground. But the guide is also designed as a pocket reference, a quick supplement to your knowledge when you are "walking the course" and need an explanation or clarification.

By far the best way to see the Fricourt area is on foot or bicycle. At the end of the text you can find a number of suggested routes making use of the paths and tracks which are accessible to these means of transport. The two chapters dealing with 1916's historic events within the designated area are obviously in chronological order. Although there was conflict here during the spring of 1918 this guide is not intended to cover that conflict in great detail since it will be the subject of a further volume in this series. However, many of the cemeteries covered by this guide contain the graves of men killed during the period March to September 1918 and I have therefore given a brief description of those events in Chapter 4. The chapter dealing with cemeteries and memorials is constructed in alphabetical order of the villages near to which those places are located.

I suggest that a tour by car or coach is the best way to get your bearings and to give an overview of the whole area. Again I have suggested a tour to highlight the main features of the area, along roads which are easily accessible. The roads covered by this suggestion are usually quite satisfactory for coaches and involve no dangerous turns through 360°! This tour is also to be found at the end of the book and is strongly recommended to those of you not already conversant with the area. It is worth noting that some of the tracks and smaller roads to be found on the IGN maps of the area are not suitable for coaches. Cars without four wheel drive will find difficulty in getting along some minor tracks, for example that leading from Fricourt to La Boisselle past Lochnagar crater. Be prepared to walk is the best advice that I can give, but do take care to lock all valuables, especially cameras and other inviting items, out of sight in the boot of your vehicle.

On the subject of Maps

Unlike the two previous villages about which I have written in this series, Thiepval and La Boisselle, the villages of Fricourt and Mametz are located firmly within just one IGN 1:25000 series map. That map is numbered 2408 est, Bray-sur-Somme. However, you would also find 2408 ouest, Albert, a useful addition since this covers all of the western approaches to the Fricourt area from the direction of Albert. For general access to the area of the Somme sheet 4 in the 1:100,000 IGN green series, Laon and Arras, is very useful. A compass is also an essential companion. For those of you interested in detail beyond the northern part of this guide Bapaume East and Bapaume West (2407 est et ouest) would also prove to be sensible purchases. Taken together these four maps cover the entirety of the British sector of the 1916 Battle of the Somme.

I have identified here the maps which appear within this guide. For most navigational and walking purposes these will be sufficient for your enjoyment of this area. However, for a really intimate knowledge of each location the 1:10,000 and 1:5,000 trench maps are indispensable to the serious student or expert. 1;10,000 maps approximate to a scale of six inches to the mile. In order to gain detailed understanding a trench map is therefore indispensable.

Map 1. The Fricourt – Mametz battlefield area, taken from the Official History's 1:40000 scale sheet. *Page 17*

Map 2. The German trenches at Fricourt, shown according to the British 1:10,000 trench map of the area corrected to 7/2/1916. *Page 28*

Map 3. The German trenches at Mametz, shown according to the British 1:10,000 trench map of the area corrected to 7/2/1916. *Page 31*

Map 4. The First Phase objectives set for the 7th and 21st Divisions. [Official History Objectives Map.] *Page 47*

Map 5. Detail from the disposition map showing the position of British units north and west of Fricourt in 50, 63 and 64 Brigade's area at zero hour on 1st July, together with their subsequent advance towards Crucifix Trench. *Page 51*

Map 6. Detail from the disposition map showing the position of the 7th Division's units south of Mametz at zero hour on 1st July. *Page 60*

Map 7. Detail from the disposition map showing the position of the 7th Green Howards and the 20th Manchesters who were involved in the Subsidiary Attack on Fricourt at 2.30 pm on 1st July 1916. *Page 67*

Map 8. German map illustrating the fighting during the 1st July along the front between La Boisselle and Mametz. *Page 70*

Map 9. Part of the Official History, Transportation on the Western Front – Map number 5, dealing with British railway lines on the Somme. *Page 74*

Map 10. German map illustrating the fighting during the 2nd July at Fricourt. *Page 79*

Map 11. Mametz Wood, 3/4th July. *Page 85*

You should note that the trench maps, which are available from the Imperial War Museum Department of Printed Books (Tel: 0171 416 5348) or the cartographer of the Western Front Association (members only), follow a specific sequence and should be referred to by the numbers usually found in their top right hand corner. Unfortunately the

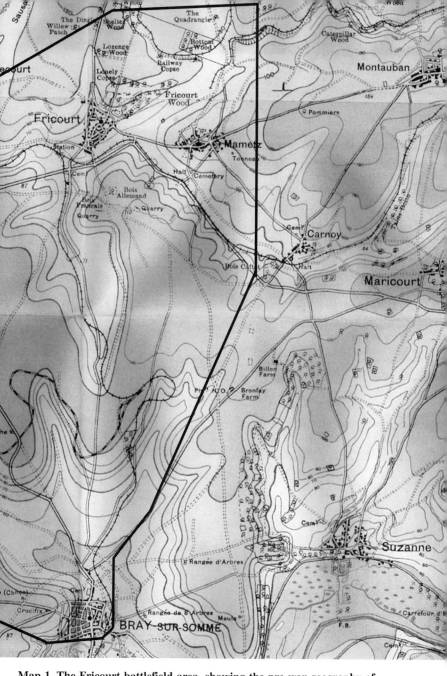

Map 1. The Fricourt battlefield area, showing the pre-war geography of the area. This is taken from the 1;40,000 sheets which accompanied the Official History volume detailing the fighting leading to the first day of the Battle of the Somme.

O. Grossel. lib. — Albei

Fricourt Chateau, 1913 and 1915.

202 — *Le Château de* FRICOURT *(Somme) après plusieurs bombardements*

CL. SEC. PH. ARM.

Visé Paris n° 351

G. Lelong, 21, Rue St-Martin, Amiens

Fricourt Chateau, 1930.

Fricourt area is covered by two sheets belonging to the 1:10,000 trench map series. Those are sheet 62d N.E.2, entitled Meaulte, which covers the village of Fricourt, and sheet 57d SE4, entitled Ovillers, which covers the higher ground to the north of Fricourt including Fricourt Farm, Shelter Wood and Bottom Wood. Variously dated versions are available from both sources. In the text I have sometimes referred to locations which are noted on such trench maps, but not on present day maps. In such cases I have where necessary given the relevant trench map reference to help you identify the exact position. For example, 'Maple Redoubt' just south of Bois Francais, was located on sheet 62d.N.E.2, at reference F.15.b.9,8.

One feature which the young or first time visitor might wish for is an easily accessible reconstruction which gives an insight into the conditions which prevailed around Fricourt at the height of the conflict. One such source of insight and empathy is to be found at Newfoundland Park, two miles north-west of Thiepval on the Auchonvillers road out of Hamel, the D73. This is an area of preserved battlefield, purchased by the government of Newfoundland after the Great War. Further detailed insight can be obtained at the two quality

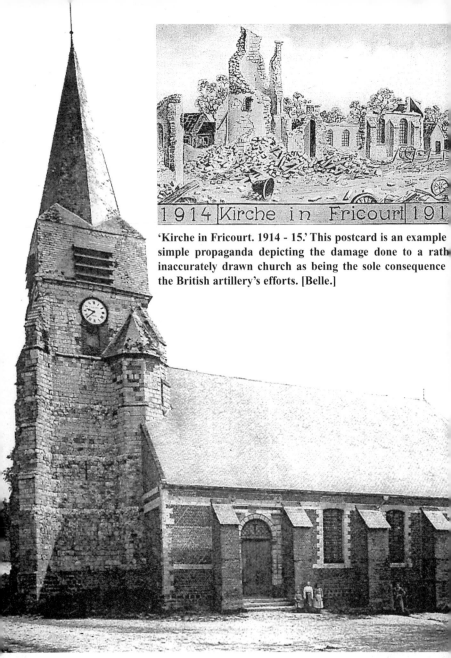

'Kirche in Fricourt. 1914 - 15.' This postcard is an example simple propaganda depicting the damage done to a rath inaccurately drawn church as being the sole consequence the British artillery's efforts. [Belle.]

The church in Fricourt village, 1913.

museums which are within reasonable distance. The first, at Albert below the celebrated Basilica, is only ten minutes away by car. The second, the "Historial" at Peronne, is well worth the longer journey, but you should remember to set aside a good forty minutes travelling time, each way. Take the D938 running south-east from Albert to Peronne, a route which will enable you to follow the southern arm of the British front lines as they existed before the opening of the battle of the Somme.

One extraordinary fact about the Somme and Ancre battlefield is that after the utter devastation of the Great War many of the tracks and other human geographical features were reconstructed in the 1920s with an uncanny similarity to their pre-war locations. Most of the pre 1914 and trench maps of the Fricourt area still stand true today. Initially the processes of reconstruction were almost insurmountably difficult. In order to help, many of the villages were adopted by some of Britain's towns and cities.

However, in the early 1920s, as more villagers returned to rebuild their homes and lives with the reparations monies wrung from Weimar

The Basilica at Albert TAYLOR LIBRARY

Germany, every effort was made to find the exact location of their pre-war houses. Sometimes, when a villager did not return that plot was left vacant, in many cases still so today! But, we should remember that Fricourt and Mametz are working villages, communities whose roots are based in centuries of toil on the land which is also our place of interest. This is not "open access" land on the National Trust model. It is all too easy to let our two interests clash. During the autumn months, in particular, be aware of the numerous shooting parties. The farmers will not welcome the sight of your tramping the fields with little regard to crops and seeds. Please ask before you enter. Please keep to the paths and the edges of each field.

Chapter One

OUR DESIGNATED AREA TODAY

The straight road which runs from Albert to Bapaume, the D929, along which it was planned to execute the 'Big Push', neatly bisects what was then the British sector of the first Battle of the Somme. However, the village of Fricourt lies a little to the south of that distinctive road. Much of the fighting north of the D929 road, in the summer, autumn and early winter of 1916 was influenced by the course of the River Ancre which has created a steeper and more substantial sequence of valleys and slopes. There is a splendid vantage point immediately to the north of Fricourt astride the spur upon which stands the Bois de Becordel, the Willow Patch, and this will give you fine views north towards La Boisselle and thence to Thiepval, as well as westwards across Becourt. Beyond Becourt, behind the battlefield, lay the town of Albert, familiar to almost every British soldier who served during the first 'Battle of the Somme'. Today Albert describes itself as being only the *"3eme Ville de la Somme"*, but quite properly *"la Cite d'Ancre"*. The Town Hall square in Albert often hosts a market and there are three small supermarkets nearby which can all provide a sound array of food and refreshments. However, the area due east of Albert past Becourt, La Boisselle and on towards Contalmaison is more undulating, gentle countryside, filled with seemingly endless fields dotted with tiny distant woods, an area within which it is easy to lose any sense of direction. The Fricourt and Mametz areas are noticeably different. Here there are many wooded areas, winding valleys, commanding heights and oppressive re-entrants. It is my

Dawn on the Somme reveals the silhouette of Fricourt village, shrouded in light mist.

sincere hope that this guidebook will provide an authoritative and interesting companion in your search for understanding and clarity.

Leaving Albert, the villages of Fricourt and Mametz can be reached from the D938 Albert to Peronne road. Fricourt and Mametz are connected by the D64, which leaves Fricourt in an easterly direction, passing through Mametz en route for Montauban. Running north to south through the village of Fricourt is the D147 road which leaves Pozieres, passing through Contalmaison and Fricourt before beginning the journey south towards Bray-sur-Somme. There are few hotels within the area covered by this guide and the first thing you might need to arrange is accommodation and tomorrow morning's breakfast. I have therefore identified below some of the nearby hotels and a number of 'English' B&B style houses where you can base yourself during a visit. However, for those of you with a tent or caravan and a more adventurous disposition, the 'Bellevue' campsite in Authuille is a fine and central point on the Somme battlefield which can be reached from Fricourt via La Boisselle in less than fifteen minutes by car. If you wish to avoid travelling back through Albert, take the D938 from Fricourt in the direction of Albert but turn off left into Becordel-Becourt. Immediately turn right into the underpass and head northwards through Becourt and beyond to La Boisselle. Cross the D929 and take the road to Aveluy which is adjacent to La Boisselle's communal cemetery. From Aveluy follow the D151 into Authuille. The campsite is quiet and often frequented by people who share an interest in the Great War. The owner, Monsieur Desailly, and his family are always welcoming. Recently the Bellevue campsite has been expanded to include a simple restaurant, reached thirty yards to the right as you look towards the main campsite entrance, where the food is both substantial and economical. Here you are within two minute's walk of the Authuille Military Cemetery and not far from the Auberge de la Vallee d'Ancre on the banks of the River Ancre. For many years this bar and restaurant has served decent food and drinks for as long as you cared to stay! The Auberge has been taken into new ownership recently (1995) by Denis Bourgoyne who has already established a fine reputation for the quality of his food amongst the local community. There is another campsite at the village of Treux in the Ancre valley south west of Albert. This alternative is pleasantly shaded from the summer's heat.

However, it can be bitterly cold camping in February! Therefore, for those of you who are travelling in style or during these colder and wetter months of the year, a roof over your heads may be welcome. The list identified below may be of some help, but it should not be inferred that the order is one of descending merit! To call for reservations from the UK dial 00 33, followed by the 9 digit number. In all these hotels, with one exception in Picquigny, you will find at least one person on the hotel's staff who can speak English.

Hotels:

The Royal Picardie ***, Route d'Amiens, 80300 Albert. Tel 322 75 37 00.
The Hotel de la Basilique **, 3 - 5 Rue Gambetta, 80300 Albert.
Tel 322 75 04 71.
The Relais Fleuri **, 56 Avenue Faidherbe, 80300 Albert.
Tel 322 75 08 11.
The Grande Hotel de la Paix *, 43 Rue Victor Hugo, 80300 Albert
Tel 322 75 01 64.
Les Etangs du Levant *, Rue du 1er Septembre, 80340 Bray sur Somme.
Tel 322 76 70 00.
Auberge de Picquigny **, 112 Rue du 60 R.I., 80310 Picquigny.
Tel 322 51 20 53.
Hotel Le Prieure. 17 Route National, 80860 Rancourt. Tel 322 85 04 43.

B&B style accommodation:

Courcelette. A distinctive family farmhouse, self catering or meals provided. 'Sommecourt' is situated right at the heart of the 1916 Somme Battlefields. Plenty of facilities including guided tours and a small but fascinating museum. This fine location provides easy access to Fricourt, less than ten minutes in a car using the D147 from Pozieres. Paul Reed and Kieron Murphy. Sommecourt, 39 Grande Rue, 80300 Courcelette. Tel: 322 74 01 35.

Auchonvillers/Beaumont Hamel. Very comfortable and well appointed accommodation for up to eight people. Attractive grounds and very interesting walks nearby. Evening meals and continental breakfast. Perhaps fifteen minutes from Fricourt driving past Newfoundland Park and Thiepval. Mike and Julie Renshaw. Les Galets. Route de Beaumont, Auchonvillers. Tel: 322 76 28 79.

Auchonvillers. Five good rooms with en suite facilities and an extremely interesting history, the centrepiece of which is the cellar still carved with the names of many soldiers who passed through in 1916. Bed, breakfast and evening meals by arrangement as well as a Tea Room for non residents. Again, access to Fricourt best undertaken by car. Avril Williams. 10 Rue Delattre, 80560 Auchonvillers. Tel: 322 76 23 66.

THE AREA OF FRICOURT AND MAMETZ

Once you are established it is time to see the surrounding locality and I suggest that, soon after you arrive, you would enjoy following the general tour explained in Chapter 6. However, in this first chapter I have attempted to give some definition to the boundaries of this guidebook and give a brief commentary to illustrate the importance of the area's history.

The upland district to the south of Fricourt has many literary associations which are of great interest and importance. Three writers in particular left immensely detailed accounts of both the fighting and the emotional experience of war which they passed through. All three served with the 1st Royal Welsh Fusiliers, Bernard Adams, Siegfried Sassoon and Robert Graves. Their battalion was part of 22 Brigade, 7th Division, which was engaged during the 1st July attacks. The books written by these three officers, *'Nothing of Importance'*, *'Memoirs of an Infantry Officer'* and *'Goodbye to All That'* were later accepted by many as the genuine experience of war. Within the pages of those three books are a multitude of insights into the complex social, military and emotional issues which swirled around the slopes and valleys of the Fricourt area in 1916.

The villages of Fricourt and Mametz are overlooked from the south by the Bois d'Engremont, known during the war as the Bois Francais and the Bois Allemand (or German Wood). The Maps supplied with the Official History are a little less than clear on the distinction between Bois Francais and Bois Allemand. Properly the Bois Francais was that part of the woods through which the French, and later the British, front line ran. That trench is identified in the British Official History as 'Aeroplane Trench', running from Fricourt's communal cemetery in a south-easterly direction until it enters the woods I have identified as Bois Francais. Bois Allemand was a small area of woodland on the east side of the sunken lane behind the German front line, in the area identified as 'Bois Francais Trench' on the Official History's maps! In order to avoid confusion I shall refer to all the woods within squares F9d and F10c as Bois Francais unless greater accuracy is required.

The front lines at Bois Francais facing north east were one of the most significant positions occupied by the French and then by British troops. The position was well known to Sassoon, Graves and Adams. From its vantage point observation could be obtained for some distance and both opposing lines running north of Fricourt were clearly visible. Another nearby location giving particularly fine panoramic

The grave of one solitary Frenchman, the reservist H.Tomassin from the class of 1900, still holds the position of Bois Francais. Around the rather ugly stonework lie the remains of many trenches.

views, south of the village of Fricourt, was the important artillery Observation Post known as Bonte Redoubt, or Point 87 (located at F.8.d), from which a perfect panorama could be viewed covering the entirety of Aeroplane Trench running up to Bois Francais, Wing Corner, Fricourt village with Mametz and Danzig Alley behind, the Tambour positions and the lines running northwards across the Fricourt spur. This Observation Post controlled the fire of guns

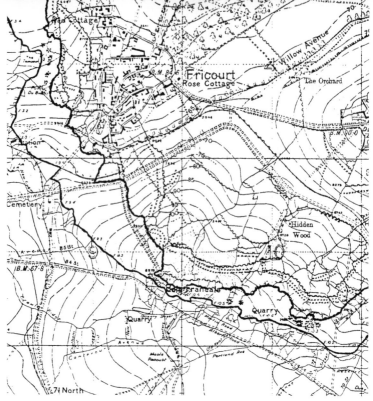

Map 2. The German trenches at Fricourt, shown according to the British 1:10,000 trench map of the area corrected to 15/6/1916.

operating from the Gibraltar positions in Happy Valley and the Bois des Tailles to the south, as well as units dug in just south of Albert to the west, all of which were therefore able to enfilade the German trenches running both north and east of Fricourt.

By contrast the British position immediately south of Bois Allemand had a very limited perspective to the north. Consequently there was an unremitting intensity to the fighting, patrolling and mining which occurred here as both sides strove to dominate the positions around Bois Francais. The reason behind this intensity was simple. The trench systems running east from Fricourt were unusual in that they were one location where the German Army had not been able, during the autumn of 1914, to establish itself along the dominant heights. Once the decision to fight the Battle of the Somme had been made it became vital that the German Army be contained in the Bois Allemand area since any German progress south would enable them to observe and dominate the British positions across the plateau running down to the Citadel and Happy Valley. Success in maintaining this higher ground south of the Albert - Peronne road was therefore one of the most significant reasons why the British troops in this sector were able to deal a more telling blow, at the outset of the First Battle of the Somme, than those troops facing German positions further north.

Today the Bonte Redoubt and Bois Francais areas provide the visitor with unrivalled panoramas. I have already suggested that a decent pair of binoculars are going to be much appreciated here as you look across a large portion of the southern sector of the Somme Battlefield.

The area dealt with by this guide is that which came under the command of XV Corps for the purposes of the attacks which took place here on 1st July 1916. Opposite XV Corps, Fricourt and Mametz formed a salient in the German positions. We can envisage the British assault at the outset of the First Battle of the Somme as taking place along an 'L' shaped front, with the village of Fricourt at the bend in that line. The Official History describes this location as, 'the corner stone of the German line between the Ancre and the Somme'. Above Fricourt the respective front lines ran roughly northwards, past Thiepval and the River Ancre, until the villages of Serre and Gommecourt. The most important British redoubt west of Fricourt was known as Queen's Redoubt, a position some 1,000 yards west of the Tambour positions. Below Fricourt the lines turned to run in an easterly direction towards Maricourt and the junction with the French Sixth Army. Behind these lines running eastwards were a series of British redoubts. The westernmost one was Bonte Redoubt with its fine panoramic view across Fricourt and northwards towards La Boisselle. East of Bonte were Reduit A, Maple Redoubt, Wellington Redoubt with Lucknow 1000 yards to the rear, and finally Minden Post. Like the other redoubts, Minden Post served as a battalion HQ both before and during the battle of the Somme, being occupied by the 21st and 22nd Manchesters and then lastly by the 1st South Staffs on 1st July. It was along the lower segment of the 'L' that the greatest progress by the British Army, in the vicinity of Mametz and especially Montauban, was made during the first day of the battle. In defining the limits of this guide to the west and north I have included the village of Meaulte, from where an imaginary line can be drawn past Becourt village continuing north-eastwards until the village of Contalmaison is reached. The line is therefore the boundary between this guide and my previous book, in this series, which deals with La Boisselle, Ovillers and Contalmaison. On the east of this guide's area the boundary lies on a line running from Minden Post and Caftet Wood, near to the village of Carnoy, northwards to the Willow Stream and the approaches to Mametz Wood. Mametz Wood itself is dealt with a separate volume. However, this guidebook also covers the ground running southwards towards the town of Bray-sur-Somme. That route south lies along the D147 and passes the site of the Citadel, where many thousands of British troops rested, recovered or died in the midst of the huge logistical effort being made to supply and maintain the impetus of the battle. The Citadel New Military Cemetery there is therefore enormously interesting and marks one of the most significant positions behind the British lines.[1]

The geography of this area had a significant impact upon the initial evolution of the battle. The villages of Fricourt and Mametz are located on two elevated spurs of higher ground, between which the valley of the Willow Stream runs (Vallee de Mametz on your IGN map). This stream drains the area of Caterpillar Wood (in the Vallee du Bois). Fricourt village lies on the south side of the western tip of the broad and rather indistinct spur which descends from the Pozieres ridge past Contalmaison where it becomes more clearly defined towards Fricourt and Becourt. Mametz lies at the western end of a rather more distinct spur running south-west from Montauban. East of Mametz Wood the Willow Stream runs along a narrow valley which lies behind the dominant German front line and support positions which ran along higher ground to the south of Mametz and Montauban. Those German positions between Mametz and Montauban were surmounted by Pommiers Redoubt which lay, just to the east of the 7th Division's attacks, on the Mametz to Montauban road. North of the Willow Stream the ground rises into the dark confines of Mametz Wood and the area of the Bazentin villages.

During the First Battle of the Somme XV Corps was commanded by Lieutenant General H.S.Horne. There were three divisions under his command; the 7th commanded by Major General H.E.Watts, the 21st commanded by Major General C.W.Jacob and the 17th, commanded by Major General T.D.Pilcher. The plan devised for the 1st July's assault placed the 21st Division on the left of XV Corps' attack, on the west of Fricourt and attacking towards the east, whilst the 7th Division attacked south of Fricourt and Mametz, moving in a northerly direction. On entering the German trenches the dividing line between the two attacking Divisions was to be the Willow Stream. It is worth noting here that 50 Brigade from the 17th Division were attached to the 21st Division for the purposes of the attacks west of Fricourt on the morning of 1st July.[2] The remainder of the 17th Division was therefore placed in corps reserve. XV Corps therefore faced a difficult challenge. Not only were there two heavily fortified villages immediately behind the German front lines, but the Corps would have to deal with the issue of simultaneously attacking in two different directions, the consequence of attacking astride a salient.

Therefore it was decided to make the assault in two phases. The main attack, timed for 7.30 am, would not fall on Fricourt. Only when progress had been secured to the north of that village and at Mametz would a subsidiary attack be implemented to pinch out the Fricourt village defences. The complexity of this plan is dealt with in greater detail in Chapter 2.

It is worth noting here that beyond the left of XV Corps' attack, when the battle commenced on 1st July 1916, stood the 34th Division, part of III Corps. Beyond the right of XV Corps' attack was the 18th Division, part of XIII Corps

1. On a contemporary trench map the Citadel can be found on sheet 62.D.NE2 at grid reference F.21.b.

2. The infantry battalions commanded by these three Divisions were as follows:

    7th Division.
        20 Brigade:
        8th Devonshire.
        9th Devonshire.

Map 3. The German trenches at Mametz, shown according to the British 1:10,000 trench map of the area corrected to 7/2/1916.

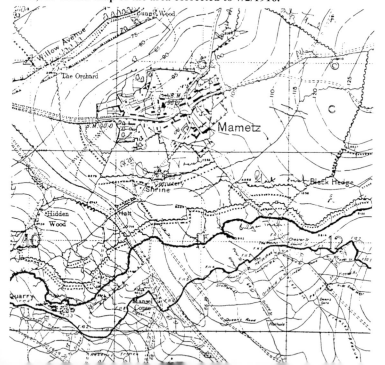

2nd Border.
2nd Gordons.

22 Brigade:
2nd Royal Warwickshire.
2nd Royal Irish.
1st Royal Welch Fusiliers.
20th Manchester (5th Manchester Pals).

91 Brigade:
2nd Queens.
1st South Staffordshires.
21st Manchesters (6th Manchester Pals).
22nd Manchesters (7th Manchester Pals).

Divisional Pioneers. 24th Manchester (Oldham).

17th (Northern) Division.

50 Brigade:
10th West Yorkshire.
7th East Yorkshire.
7th Green Howards.
6th Dorsetshire.

51 Brigade:
7th Lincolnshire.
7th Border.
8th South Staffordshire.
10th Sherwood Foresters.

52 Brigade:
9th Northumberland Fusiliers.
10th Lancashire Fusiliers.
9th Duke of Wellingtons.
12th Manchesters.

Divisional Pioneers: 7th York and Lancasters.

21st Division.

62 Brigade:
12th Northumberland Fusiliers.
13th Northumberland Fusiliers.
1st Lincolnshire.
10th Green Howards.

63 Brigade:
8th Lincolnshires.
8th Somerset Light Infantry.
4th Middlesex.
10th York and Lancasters.

64 Brigade:
1st East Yorkshires.
9th K.O.Y.L.I.
10th K.O.Y.L.I.
15th Durham Light Infantry.

Divisional Pioneers: 14th Northumberland Fusiliers.

Chapter Two

THE BRITISH PERSPECTIVE TO JULY 1916

Arrival!

Whilst the soldiers of his 7th Division became familiar with the landscape, south of Mametz and Fricourt, Bernard Adams, serving with the 1st Royal Welsh Fusiliers, laughed at the precarious wooden structure which was his establishment in Trafalgar Square, just south of the Bois Francais.[1] He referred to this dug-out as the Summer House, or the Straw Palace, because of the inadequate protection which its previous occupants, the French, had developed. Adams speaks of his position overlooking the shattered copse as,

> 'the maddest so called 'dug-out' in the British lines ..... for the French, although they presumably built it in the summer days of 1915 when the Bois Francais trenches were a sort of summer-rest for tired-out soldiers, would never have tolerated the 'Summer-house' since the advent of the canister age.'[2]

Robert Graves, in his book *Goodbye to All That*, spoke of the multitude of rats which infested the dugouts near Bois Francais above Fricourt.

> 'It was an even worse place than Cuinchy for rats; they

Schloss Fricourt. The postcard was drawn in November 1914 and reproduced in quantity. This example was posted in April 1915 and reveals the far less restrictive attitude which Germany's Army had to the issue of identifying where its soldiers were based. [Belle.][3]

German trenches at Point 110.

scuttled about 'A' Company mess at meal-times. We always ate with revolvers beside our plates, and punctuated our conversation with sudden volleys at a rat rummaging at somebody's valise or crawling along the timber support of the roof above our heads.'

At night, when conditions allowed, Adams and his fellow officers slept in a dug-out a little way further back in Old Kent Road, at F.10.c.5,1, a communication trench running south-westwards back towards Maple Redoubt. Any unit garrisoning the trenches south of Bois Francais used Maple Redoubt as the Battalion HQ. To aid navigation in the warren of subterranean passages all the communication trenches in this area were numbered, 66 Street being east of Mansell Copse thence via 67 through to 80 Street south of Bois Francais and beyond. The constant process of damage and repair to these fragile forms of shelter taxed the pioneer soldiers from Oldham, the 24th Manchesters, considerably. On the night of 23rd May for example this battalion's A Company was engaged in much night work maintaining the structure of the positions south-west of Mansell Copse. The trench known as Dale Street, referred to in the quotation below, crosses the lane running past the Devons' cemetery at Mansell Copse some 120 yards up the slope above the copse.

'26 other ranks deepening trench mortar emplacements off Wellington Avenue. Five other ranks dug trench 4.5 yards, connecting 69 St. and Suffolk Avenue. Eight other ranks revetted traverses in Dale St. Thirty other ranks revetted 14 fire bays in Lucknow Avenue. Forty five other ranks carried 270 pickets, 3,000 yards barbed wire, 500 sandbags; revetted parapet of strong point; levelled and covered parados; worked on three mined dug-outs, and communication trench - 45 yards.' [4]

Night after night the work was never ending, the consequence of reciprocal destruction wrought by the artillery, the trench mortar teams and the miners of both sides. Yet here, astride the much contested high ground above Fricourt and Mametz, the craters left by the detonation of mines gave the winter's moonlit nights an eerie quality. Bernard Adams wrote evocatively about the scene after he had made one of his many tours to witness the sentries, sand-baggers and wiring parties at work in the moon's half harsh light.

'Craters by moonlight are really beautiful; the white chalk-dust gives them the appearance of snow mountains. And they look much larger than they really are. On this occasion, as I looked into them from the various bombing-posts, it needed little imagination to suppose I was up in the snows of the Welsh hills. There was such a death-like stillness over it all, too. The view from the Matterhorn was across the widest and deepest of all the craters, and I stood a long time peering across that yawning chasm at the dark, irregular rim of German sandbags. I gazed fascinated. What was it all about? The sentry beside me came from a village near Dolgelly: was a farmer's boy. He, too, was gazing across, hardly liking to shuffle his feet, lest he broke the silence.'

One saddening event in the Fricourt area, which brought two prominent writers together, was the death of 2nd Lieutenant David Thomas on 18th March. Thomas was a personal friend of both Robert Graves and Siegfried Sassoon. 'A' Company, 1st RWF, had been working from seven in the evening through till midnight. The men had placed upwards of 3,000 sandbags in position south of Bois Francais to strengthen the front lines when, about 10.30 pm, rifle fire had broken out. David Thomas was hit in the neck but initially seemed well, walking to the dressing station. Soon after his arrival at the dressing station and fearing that he would not survive his wounds Thomas had given a letter to an orderly, written for despatch to a girl in Glamorgan in the event of his death. Moments later David Thomas had begun to choke and the doctor had tried tracheotomy but to no avail. It was some hours before Robert Graves heard the galling news that Thomas had died; he felt the death of his friend more deeply than any other since his arrival in France. But when Siegfried Sassoon heard of Thomas's death on 19th March he was deeply angered.

Both Graves and Sassoon attended the burial at the Point 110 (new) cemetery. Sassoon's diary described the scene which was repeated many times on this plot of downland above Fricourt.

'In the half clouded moonlight the parson stood above the graves, and everything was dim but the striped flag laid across them. Robert Graves, beside me, with his white whimsical face twisted and grieving. Once we could not hear the solemn words for the noise of a machine-gun along the line; when all was finished a canister fell a few hundred yards away to burst with a crash'

Later the following day Sassoon escaped to the woods above the banks of the Somme at Sailly-Laurette to be alone with his grief. Graves tells how, in the weeks after the event, having brought the battalion's rations up every evening in his capacity as Acting Transport Officer, Sassoon would go out into No Man's Land on patrol 'looking for Germans to kill.'

Perhaps one of the most graphically vivid descriptions of military action, here at Bois Francais, has therefore been left by Sassoon who wrote self effacingly about the events which led to his being awarded the Military Cross. The date was 26th May 1916 when twenty seven men together with one officer, their faces blackened, nerves taut and courage braced, left Maple Redoubt across the open towards 77 Street, one of the communication trenches which linked with the front line near to the quarry east of the Bois Allemand woods. Sassoon had been denied permission to accompany the raiding parties, perhaps because of his reputation for recklessness. After midnight he sat on the British parapet, waiting. At first he sat in silence, then listening almost disinterestedly as increasing numbers of 5.9s began to drone across the skies. He moved forward a little way and after twenty minutes out in No Man's Land Sassoon heard that the raiders were held up

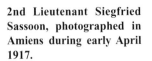

2nd Lieutenant Siegfried Sassoon, photographed in Amiens during early April 1917.

36

by the depth of German wire. One man told him that Corporal O'Brien said 'it's a failure'. Within seconds a fierce fire fight broke out and the craters spumed showers of water as dozens of grenades were thrown. Having counted sixteen men back Sassoon then went out to see if he could recover any more of the wounded. This he did, in the face of intense and almost point blank fire in the pitch darkness. On a number of occasions before the dawn Sassoon went out, taking other men with him, to collect the wounded. His most difficult task was the rescue of Corporal O'Brien who lay about twenty five feet down in a crater to the right of the raiding party's positions. O'Brien was badly wounded and it took an enormous effort of both strength and willpower to attempt the rescue.

'I get a rope and two more men and we go back to O'Brien, who is unconscious now. With great difficulty we get him half-way up the face of the crater; it is now after one o'clock and the sky beginning to get lighter. I make one more journey to our trench for another strong man and to see to a stretcher being ready. We get him in, and it is found that he has died, as I feared.'

Later, as the weather warmed and early June's summer nights seemed interminably long, Adams wrote of watching a British bombardment fall on the C2 sector at the southern end of Fricourt village. He had walked along Park Lane, a communication trench running north from Maple Redoubt, at F.15.b.9,8, towards its junction with Watling Street, at F.9.d.85,15, where the 1st RWF maintained a Lewis gun position. From there Adams, a fellow officer whom he called Owen, and Lance Corporal Allan[5] watched as a storm of gun flashes to the rear was translated into a succession of flickering blue and orange bursts as the shells crashed relentlessly into the German trenches. Lance Corporal Allen was enthused by the sight and smiled.

'.... and as he did so the flashes lit up his face. He was quite a boy, only eighteen, I believe, but an excellent NCO. He had a very beautiful though sensuous face that used to remind me sometimes of the 'Satyr' of Praxiteles. His only fault was an inclination to sulkiness at times, which was perhaps due to a little streak of vanity. It was no wonder the maidens of Morlancourt made eyes at him, and a little girl who lived next-door to the Lewis-gunner's billet was said to have lost her heart long ago. Tonight I felt a pang as I saw him smile.'

In the brightness of early morning, Tuesday 6th June, the British and German mortar teams and artillery exchanged further blows, retaliation, around Bois Francais. Within minutes Bernard Adams

German troops in Fricourt during the winter of 1915.

came across the scene where one small tragedy had been enacted and later felt the remorse at reporting the vileness of war in such stark and naked detail.

'In the trench, half buried in rags of sand-bag and loose chalk, lay what had been a man. His head was nearest to me, and at that I gazed fascinated; for the shell had cut it clean in half, and the face lay like a mask, its features unmarred at all, a full foot away from the rest of the head. The flesh was grey, that was all; the eyes open, the nose, the mouth were not even twisted awry. It was like a fragment of a sculpture. All the rest of the body was mangled mass of flesh and khaki.'

Looking up towards Point 110 from behind the German lines near to Fricourt communal cemetery. May 1916.

Later, when Adams reported the terrible event to Edwards, the Lewis-Coy officer, Edwards' only thoughts were for the women who would bear the anguish.

'How will they tell his little girl in Morlancourt? What will she say when she learns she will never see him again?'

A Raid on Bulgar Point, 2nd June 1916, by the 22nd Manchesters

I have taken the substance of this event from my book which deals with the service of the Manchester Pals.[6] Three Pals battalions from Manchester, the 20th, 21st and 22nd, served within the 7th Division, and the Oldham 'Comrades', or 24th Manchesters as they are properly known, were the 7th Division's pioneers.[7] In order to get to the scene where this raid was carried out locate The Mound which is approximately 500 metres along the Mametz lane which runs north-westwards from Carnoy. This is where the British front line trench crossed the lane. It was faced here by Bulgar Trench. Bulgar Point lay 300 metres due west of The Mound.

The raid by A Company of the 22nd Manchesters, undertaken on Bulgar Point at 11.00 pm on 2nd June, was typical of the many small scale actions whose justification was the acquisition of enemy disposition details. Bulgar Point was a German listening post located in a sap jutting out into No Man's Land south of Mametz. Its location was F.11.b.3,1 and arrangements were already in hand to undermine and blow up this position when the battle was commenced. Nevertheless, as that forthcoming battle approached it was still imperative to have up to date information about the enemy's dispositions as well as the nature of his defences and the strength of his protection. For five weeks prior to their raid the 22nd Manchester's men rehearsed on a model of the German trenches dug behind the British lines, south of Bronfay Farm. The raiding party consisted of sixty men, twenty in a covering party and forty who would enter the German trenches with the intention of wreaking havoc and taking prisoners. Lieutenant Oldham was in command, the covering party being led by 2nd Lieutenant Joshua Cansino. Before the raid a substantial bombardment took place, lasting for forty minutes, using howitzers, 60 pounders, 18 pounders and trench mortars. The assembly of the men was organised at Minden Post, from where they moved before exiting the British lines at F.11.d.2,7. Their entry into the German trench was undertaken without real difficulty apart from the need to force gaps in the wire. Five large dugouts containing an unknown number of men were bombed and fifteen further Germans were killed in the nearby trenches. Lieutenant Oldham remained at the point of entry just west of Bulgar Point whilst his second in command, 2nd Lieutenant Street, went further forward with the bombers. These men took four prisoners belonging to the 23rd Silesian Regiment, two of whom were killed because they offered resistance. Everything was going according to plan.

Unfortunately the withdrawal was less successful. Considerable delay was experienced as the men searched for the gaps in the wire. Within seconds the Germans were able to bring a machine gun to bear and bombs began to fall around the men. 2nd Lieutenant Edmund Street was seen to be stuck fast on the wire. Alfred Bland, A Company commander, was devastated when his returning men brought news of what had happened.

"I have borrowed two B Coy Officers. It's extraordinary. All the original A Coy Officers are gone, and I alone am left. Yes, at one blow we have lost four officers, three killed and Oldham wounded. Street, Burchill and Cansino are dead. Oldham, Street and Cansino with sixty NCO's and men raided the German trenches opposite on Friday night last. They had been practising the show for three weeks and all was arranged, every man to his task, perfect in every detail. As a show it was a success. They did considerable damage, secured two prisoners and dealt destruction to a great many more. The only hitch was the enemy wire, which had not been cut by the Artillery preparation. Street, as last to leave the Bosche trench, ran greatest risks, and got fast on the wire. Burchill went across to help him and received a fatal stomach wound, and Cansino did likewise and, so far as we

German trench near Mametz 1916.

Lieutenant Joshua Cansino, killed in action on 2/6/1916 during a raid on the German positions opposite the 22nd Manchester's trenches. Cansino was a graduate of Manchester University. He had spent a year in Berlin researching and teaching during progress towards his M.Sc. degree but when war broke out he was living in Paris, returning to England to enlist as a private in the Royal Sussex Regiment. Having quickly reached the rank of sergeant he was commissioned into the 22nd Manchesters, in November 1915, and posted to France in March 1916. As his great friend Alfred Bland says in his letter, Joshua Cansino's body was not recovered and his name is therefore commemorated on the Thiepval memorial. [Greenhill]

know, was killed in attempting to save Street. The two latter have not been recovered. Oldham is all right, with a "blighty" in the shoulder. Six men are missing. The Officer casualties are appallingly heavy, but the task attempted was magnificently accomplished. We mourn our three beyond speech. Street leaves a widow and three children. Cansino a widow and an unborn babe...." (Captain Alfred Bland. 4/6/1916)

Immediately before the Battle of the Somme, when out of the lines, the 21st and 22nd Manchesters found themselves in the Bois des Tailles near to Bray. Whilst here their rest days were not taken as labour for the Tunnelling Companies working at Bois Francais, as were the 5th City Battalion's men. However, the 6th and 7th Pals' men were, more often than not, put to work on the new metre gauge railway lines being prepared in the vicinity of the Citadel, in readiness for the "Big Push".

The Miners

Whilst the most visible and spectacular consequence of British mining on the Western Front has been preserved nearby, at Lochnagar, the German front lines around Fricourt and Mametz were also to be subject to a considerable effort of the part of the Royal Engineers' Tunnelling Companies. The most notable was undertaken by the 178th Tunnelling Company who placed three mines in readiness under the German lines opposite a British position known as the Tambour, due west of Fricourt. Collectively these three mines amounted to almost 50,000 pounds of ammonal. [8] The purpose of these mines was to throw up lips which would prevent any enfilade fire from the German

Tambour positions, located at F.3.c.5,7, across the advance of the 21st Division north of Fricourt. This whole area was a veritable warren of shafts and tunnels which had already produced a patchwork of small craters in this area.

Other locations subjected to the attentions of the miners were the trench lines running east from the heights of Bois Francais. Before the summer of 1916 No Man's Land south of Bois Francais had already witnessed the blowing of at least eight mines. Five hundred yards to the east of the woods the area of Kiel and Danube trenches had also already been subjected to extensive mining operations. Since this area south of Fricourt, including all of the sunken lane from Wing Corner to Bois Francais and east to Kiel Trench, was not to be subjected to a frontal assault during 1st July's attacks, the miners made similar preparations to those west of Fricourt. During the Subsidiary Attack made later during the day, this line from Wing Corner to positions east of Bois Francais would provide the 20th Manchesters with the dubious distinction of having the longest battalion frontage to cope with during any attack made on 1st July! Therefore three mines were to be sprung at Kiel Trench and one at Danube Trench, with two intended outcomes. The first was the intention of protecting the left of the 7th Division's initial attack south of Mametz. The second was to protect the 20th Manchesters during the second phase Subsidiary Attack.

Finally a 2,000 pound charge was laid beneath Bulgar Point, facing the 1st South Staffs' attack, together with a smaller charge of 200 pounds under a sap to the west, facing the 2nd Gordon Highlanders' attack. On the extreme right of the 7th Division's frontage two small charges of 500 pounds each were laid beneath Austrian Trench, on the boundary with XIII Corps' sphere of action, where the 22nd Manchesters would be the 7th Divisions right hand assault battalion.[9]

Final Preparations

The plan which had been agreed made the assault upon Fricourt one of the more innovative and complex actions undertaken on 1st July 1916. This was necessary since the German defences here were, as we have seen, of exceptional strength. Behind the front line there existed a maze of fire and communication trenches some twelve hundred yards in depth. The front line trench snaked back and forth creating many salients and flanks which were ideally suited to defence. The villages of Fricourt and Mametz had been turned into self contained fortifications and the German dugouts were later found to be of great depth, in some cases of two stories, and usually supplied with

A German soldier poses with a field telephone near to the entrance of Heblen Tunnel, within Fricourt, during 1915-16.

electricity. Behind the German front line there existed two significant intermediate positions. The first was sited approximately 1,000 yards behind the villages and consisted of Fritz Trench, Railway Alley and Crucifix Trench. The second, a further 1,000 yards to the rear, surrounded the approaches to Mametz Wood and included White Trench, Wood Trench and Quadrangle Trench and constituted the main

A typically substantial dugout, discovered in the Fricourt Mametz sector.

German Second Position in this area (see map). Any frontal attack upon Fricourt would, it was generally agreed, be likely to fail in the face of heavy casualties.

The attack would therefore be divided into two phases. During the first, which would take place at 7.30 am, the higher ground north of Fricourt village on Fricourt spur would be attacked and captured by the left brigade of the 21st Division, who would then continue their advance until reaching Bottom Wood where they would, hopefully, join up with the right brigade of the 7th Division. The centre brigade of the 21st Division would form a defensive flank facing the northern side of Fricourt. However, the strong defences at Fricourt and Fricourt Wood were to be left isolated. On the other side of the Willow Stream gap Mametz village would also be attacked at 7.30. by the right brigade of the 7th Division. The advance of this brigade would also bring them to the vicinity of Bottom Wood, leaving the centre brigade to form a defensive flank along the southern bank of the Willow Stream facing Fricourt and its wood. The village of Fricourt would thus, if all went according to plan, be surrounded. Therefore, the inner brigades of both divisions were ordered to wait in their front line and support trenches until, as the Official History put it, 'the situation created by the advance of the others was favourable for the attack to be launched against Fricourt, the hour for which would be settled by the corps commander.'[10] Here in the vicinity of Fricourt and Mametz the idea that this sector of the Battle of the Somme was opened with an unbroken line of British soldiers walking forward, rifles at the slope, is completely inaccurate.

It is also worth noting here that the 21st Division had suffered a disastrous start to their fighting career in France. During the Battle of Loos (September 1915) these relatively poorly trained and completely inexperienced New Army troops had been exposed to a very severe baptism of fire[11] during which they had incurred terrible casualties and also acquired a reputation for ill discipline in the face of enemy fire. Such a perception did little justice to the bravery of the men who had been badly led at Loos. The officer commanding the 9th KOYLI, Lieutenant Colonel Colmer William Lynch, had subsequently become particularly unpopular with his fellow battalion officers, as a consequence of the way he had treated them after the Loos fiasco. Lieutenant Colonel Lynch was the son of a military marriage, his father being Major General William Wiltshire Lynch, CB, and Colonel Lynch's disdainful manner had not endeared him to the many 'temporary gentlemen' who now populated his battalion's officers' mess. Before the Battle of the Somme a number of these officers had put in for transfer, some even to the notoriously dangerous Kite Balloon Section. At a final meal two days before the battle a number of officers had pointedly refused to participate in a toast which had linked the regiment with the CO's name. Fortunately the situation was rescued by Captain Haswell who proposed. 'Gentlemen, I give you the toast of the King's Own Yorkshire Light Infantry, and in particular the 9th Battalion of the Regiment,' at which moment Haswell paused for thought, 'Gentlemen, when the barrage lifts ......'[12]

The German troops who would have to withstand and repel this assault were men of the 28th Reserve Division. Opposite the 7th Division, on the right of XV Corps' attack, were the greater part of 109 Reserve Regiment. This unit had their 1st and 3rd Battalions, together with 15 machine guns, in the front lines and nearby scattered shell hole positions. The 2nd Battalion were in support in and around the Danzig Alley trench, just east of Mametz. Opposite the 21st Division, west of Fricourt, was the 111th Reserve Regiment.

The British artillery bombardment of these areas had produced a number of discernible and militarily significant effects. During the days leading up to 1st July a substantial proportion of the German 28th Division's artillery had been caught by British counter battery fire. On 1st July so many guns had been put out of action that the Germans were, as the day unfolded, unable to prevent the free movement of reinforcements from getting forward in the Mametz area. The effective use of the Royal Flying Corps' aeroplanes as artillery spotters also meant that, on 1st July, the German machine guns in Danzig Alley and other positions north of Mametz were destroyed by direct hits.

Although the German dugouts in the front lines were still intact, the German troops had not been able to complete the construction of more dugouts to the rear. As a consequence, when the assault began, many German troops were crowded into front line positions south of Mametz and their defence lacked the necessary depth. Opposite the 21st Division the physical destruction was even more difficult for the 111th Reserve Regiment's men. Here the trenches, obstacles, observation posts and weaker dugouts were almost completely destroyed and only the deepest and strongest shelters had survived. On Fricourt spur above the village the damage position and casualty figures were catastrophic. One company of the 110th Reserve Regiment had here been reduced to just eighty men by the effects of the British bombardment. Unfortunately, 'the amount of damage done to Fricourt by the bombardment had been small on account of the failure of the 9.2-inch shells to explode, the fuzes having come out during flight.'[13]

Much of the credit for the early success achieved at Mametz and Fricourt must go to the artillery barrage planning, undertaken by XV Corps, which was meticulous. Interestingly, after the war these plans were reproduced in full within the Official History as an object lesson in thorough planning.[14] The orders for the preliminary barrage were issued by XV Corps' CRA, Brigadier General E.W. Alexander, on 12th June. Those orders detailing the final concentrated, and subsequent creeping, barrages were issued on 14th June. Once the attack was underway, whilst the heavy guns would lift back at intervals, the 18 pounder guns would search back across the German positions by progressively increasing their range. The instructions issued by

A view in Mametz after the bombardment. TAYLOR LIBRARY

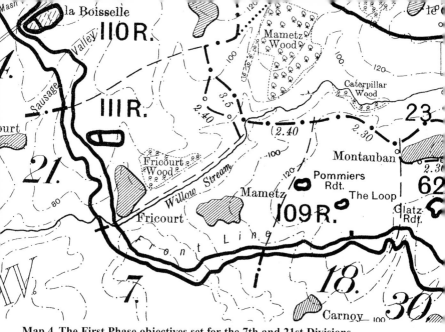

Map 4. The First Phase objectives set for the 7th and 21st Divisions.

Brigadier General J.G.Rotton, CRA of the 7th Division, made plain that,

> 'During the advance of the infantry a barrage of artillery fire will be formed in front of the infantry. ...... The divisional artillery will move their fire progressively at the rate of 50 yards a minute. Should the infantry arrive at any point before the time fixed for the barrage to lift, they will wait under the best cover available and be prepared to assault directly the lift takes place.'

Parallel instructions issued to the infantry made clear that,

> 'The line of the barrage must be constantly watched by the infantry, whose front lines must keep close up to it.' [War Diary. 15th D.L.I.]

The final intensive bombardment of the Fricourt salient area began at 6.25 on the morning of July 1st. In those locations where no initial assault was to be made a quantity of gas was released between 7.15 and 7.25 am. In the midst of the gas release, at 7.22 am, a hurricane bombardment by the Stokes mortars of both divisions took place. Four minutes later smoke was discharged in order to screen the inner flanks of the attacking brigades to the north of Fricourt and south of Mametz. At 7.28 the mines at the Tambour and elsewhere were all detonated simultaneously. Unfortunately the creeping barrage idea, referred to above, was not extended to covering No Man's Land so the attacking troops drew no benefit from the idea as they crossed between the

47

opposing front lines at the start of the infantry assault.

I have described these events in a series of snapshots, starting on the left of XV Corps' front and moving towards the right and its junction with XIII Corps. As we have noted, the assault would be undertaken by the 21st Division on the left flank, consisting of 62, 63 and 64 Brigades, along with 50 Brigade attached from the 17th Division which was in corps reserve. On the right was the 7th Division, consisting of 91, 20 and 22 Brigades.

The assault made on Fricourt on the morning of 1st July (21st Division)

Although the artillery planning was meticulous the execution proved that the concept of the Creeping Barrage still had to undergo a considerable evolution before becoming the principal weapon of the successful infantry advances which were seen at the end of the war from August 1918 onwards. In the event the barrage proved to be rather too thin, only shrapnel being fired, and too fast moving for the infantry to keep up with.

1) 64 Brigade's attack towards Crucifix Trench

64 Brigade's attack took place from positions due east of Becourt. For easy access from the centre of Fricourt walk north along the D147 until you can turn left, two hundred yards before you reach the German cemetery. After 250 yards take the right fork which leads uphill towards the higher ground of Fricourt spur. As you cross the highest point ignore the track on your right which leads up towards the Willow Patch. Walk ahead, until you reach the track on your left after 100 yards. This point marks the exact location of the German front line here. South Sausage Trench ran due north from here towards the Heligoland Redoubt which overlooked Sausage Valley. Keep to the right and begin the steady descent into Sausage Valley. Here the track lies in No Man's Land across which the 8th Somerset Light Infantry attacked on 1st July. Further down the slope, attacking towards South Sausage Trench 250 yards to your right, were the 9th and 10th KOYLI. Beyond the 10th KOYLI were the soldiers of the 34th Division.

To help understand the attacks here you should note that west and north-west of Fricourt the 21st Division placed three brigades in the line. 64 Brigade was, as we have seen, on the left adjacent to the men of the 34th Division. 63 Brigade was in the centre and on their left were 50 Brigade, facing Fricourt. 50 Brigade was not due to attack initially, but the 10th West Yorks were due to advance to form the defensive flank north of the village. The attack of the 64th Brigade was also assisted by three 18 pounder batteries of the 95th Brigade, RFA, who were dug in on the southernmost strip of Becourt Wood (adjacent to Norfolk Cemetery). Before zero the men of the 9th and 10th KOYLI crept out into No Man's Land and advanced as soon as the barrage lifted. Facing them the Germans had placed machine guns in their front lines and were also able to enfilade the ground from the Horseshoe Trench and Scots Redoubt positions on the higher ground of the Fricourt spur. Here the German wire had been well cut and the German positions were overrun as the KOYLI and their support battalions, the 15th DLI and the 1st East Yorks, mingled into a formidable force within the German positions. During the next few minutes 64 Brigade's men fought their way eastwards until, by 8.00 am, they were in control of the Sunken Lane, today the D147 Contalmaison road, from where further advances were made to Crucifix Trench facing Shelter Wood. However, machine gun fire from Fricourt, Shelter and Birch Tree Woods made further progress untenable. The situation was further complicated by the failure of the 34th Division on their left. By this time, 8.05 am, the brigade's only surviving commanding officer was Lieutenant Colonel A.E.Fitzgerald of the 15th DLI[15].

Fitzgerald was placed in charge of the defence of this area by the Brigade Commander, Brigadier General Headlam, who had made his way forward to the Sunken Lane. Headlam ordered more support for the parties in Crucifix Trench and sent Lewis Gun teams to hold Lozenge Wood to the south. Headlam himself led an attack on Round Wood which was still in German hands, but during the reconnaissance the Brigade Major, G.B.Bosanquet, was killed. Headlam then ordered a halt to any further attempts to advance in view of the lack of support to either flank. At this point in the fighting the left flank of the 21st Division's advance was situated at X.21.d.6,6 where Crucifix Trench crossed the Sunken Lane. It was at this moment that two battalions of the 21st Division's reserve, the 10th Yorks (Green Howards) and the 1st Lincolns were sent forward. The 10th Green Howards moved forward from the original British trenches opposite Empress Trench and Ball Lane, then moving forward across Lozenge Trench and the sunken lane until parties of the survivors reached Crucifix Trench north of Lozenge Wood. Meanwhile, the 1st Lincolns moved to the extreme left of the 21st Division's position. It was during the engagement of the 10th Green Howards that afternoon, north of Fricourt, that the Victoria Cross was won by Major Stewart Walter Loudoun-Shand (see the entry in Chapter 5, Norfolk Cemetery).

2) 63 Brigade and the 10th West Yorks

For a clear view of the scene upon which these events were enacted you can do no better than to walk to the Fricourt New Military Cemetery a few yards north-west of the Tambour mines. From the centre of Fricourt walk north along the D147 until you can turn left, two hundred yards before you reach the German cemetery. The houses on your left as you walk up the lane away from the D147 are the location of Red Cottage, west of which lay Red Trench which was an important German support position. After 250 yards take the left fork. Here you are 150 yards behind the German front line, Konig Trench. The path to the British cemetery is a further 50 yards along, on the left, the cemetery therefore being constructed a few yards north of the British Tambour positions, in a location across which the 10th West Yorks attacked on 1st July 1916.

The attack of 63 Brigade and the 10th West Yorks took place along the 800 yards of lines north of the Tambour position. The mines under the German positions were detonated at 7.28 am. To the north, on the left of 63 Brigade's attack, the German front line known as Empress Trench was assaulted by the 8th Somerset Light Infantry, who immediately came under heavy machine gun fire as soon as they crept forward before zero hour. Nevertheless, their attack was delivered successfully, albeit with heavy casualties, and groups of men managed to advance past the German support trench, but not as far as the Sunken Lane on the right of 64 Brigade's advance. On the Somerset men's right the 4th Middlesex were exposed to a terrible ordeal. As soon as they had crawled forward, five minutes before zero, they had been hit by such a weight of machine gun fire that the whole battalion had been forced to withdraw. They were immediately reorganised into just one line and sent forward again at 7.29. On rising to attack this gallant band became the target for no less than six machine guns, two just behind the German front line in Konig Trench and four sited near to Red Cottage, at F.3.a.9,6. Of the men belonging to the two attacking companies about forty pressed on until they reached the Sunken Lane. The survivors of the two support companies, about one hundred men, secured the German front lines north of Fricourt under the command of Lieutenant Colonel H.P.F. Bicknell.

Siegfried Sassoon, serving at this time with C Coy, 1st RWF, was particularly well placed to observe these events and witness the severity of the German machine-gun fire. His company was drawn up behind the 20th Manchesters in Sandown Avenue, south-west of Wing Corner. In his *Memoirs of an Infantry Officer* Sassoon describes how

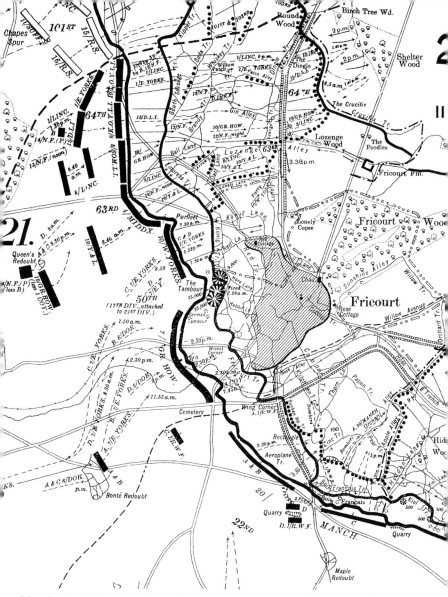

Map 5. Detail from the disposition map showing the position of British units north and west of Fricourt in 50, 63 and 64 Brigade's area at zero hour on 1st July, together with their subsequent advance towards Crucifix Trench.

his dug-out was being shaken by the impact of 5.9 shells. 'Barton and I sat speechless, deafened and stupefied by the seismic state of affairs, and when I lit a cigarette the match flame staggered crazily.' As the 7th Division's attack got underway, Sassoon left the shelter of the dug-out and went up the stairs to observe the scene from Kingston Road Trench. Sassoon's position was thus a little to the east of Bonte Redoubt, close to the junction between Kingston Road and Sandown Avenue at F.9.c.2,9, from where he had a clear view across the communal cemetery into Fricourt, across the Willow Stream valley towards Fricourt Wood and the spur, as well as towards the Tambour positions. His description of the events which began at 7.30 am is, as expected, immensely vivid.

> 'The air vibrates with the incessant din - the whole earth shakes and rocks and throbs - it is one continuous roar. Machine-guns tap and rattle, bullets whistling overhead - small fry quite undone by the gangs of hooligan-shells that dash over to rend the German lines with their demolition-parties.'

Fifteen minutes later Sassoon's description continued, noting that the British barrage was moving to the right, eastwards, across his line of vision.

> 'The artillery barrage is now working to the right of Fricourt and beyond. I have seen the 21st Division advancing on the left of Fricourt; and some Huns apparently surrendering - about three quarters of a mile away. Our men advancing steadily to the first line. A haze of smoke drifting across the landscape - brilliant sunshine. Some Yorkshires on our left [these were men of the 10th Yorks] watching the show and cheering as if at a football match.'

But in 63 Brigade's headquarters the forward movement of the support battalions, which had been expected to capture Bottom Wood and Quadrangle Trench, was being delayed. However, within minutes it was realised that the 8th Somersets and 4th Middlesex had lost so heavily that they might not be able to hold any ground gained. Therefore, at 8.40 am, the 10th York & Lancs along with the 8th Lincolns were sent forward, only themselves to suffer heavy casualties in crossing No Man's Land as they moved up the Fricourt spur. These battalions' men, along with the remnants of the assault battalions, then pressed forward until reaching the Sunken Road north of Fricourt, where bombing duels were fought throughout the day as parties of German bombers attempted to push northwards along Lonely Trench (immediately opposite the site of the German cemetery on the D147).

South of the Middlesex and 10th York and Lancs battalions the picture was even bleaker. Here the 10th West Yorks made their ill fated attack, just north of the British Tambour position, at 7.30 am. South of the Tambour the British front lines were held by the 7th Yorks (Green

Howards) who, it was planned, would attack along with the 20th Manchesters during the Subsidiary Attack anticipated later in the day. The 10th West Yorks therefore had no troops on their right flank, but the detonation of the mines under the German Tambour position would, it was believed, protect the right flank of the West Yorks battalion. Striking eastwards, it was set the task of capturing the northern portion of the village and a length of the lane leading from there in the direction of Contalmaison. For an alternative perspective on this attack it is also possible to visualise these events clearly from the embankment, adjacent to the large German cemetery, just north of Fricourt today. As the 10th West Yorks attack began all initially went well, since the Germans were slow to emerge from their deep dug-outs. The two leading companies crossed the German front lines, Konig Trench, with relatively little loss, pressing on towards Red Cottage. However, the two support companies were faced with a different proposition. By the time these men advanced the machine-guns in the northern part of the German Tambour had been brought into action, as had those guns near Red Cottage. The barrage was now distant and there was simply no British fire to keep the German soldiers within Fricourt under cover. The Official History gives an unusually lengthy description of these events.

> '..... the third and fourth companies were practically annihilated and shot down in their waves. Lieutenant Colonel A.Dickson and all the regimental staff, including the second-in-command and adjutant, were killed, and only small groups reached the German front trench. The leading companies, however, passed on along the communication trenches and

Siegfried Sassoon's position, from which he witnessed the events at Fricourt on 1st July 1916, lay at the junction of Kingston Road and Sandown Avenue, just beyond the farm in the centre of this photograph, which was taken from the slopes south-west of Bois Francais. The important artillery observation post known as Bonte Redoubt lay further past Sassoon's position on the left of the lane leading westwards away from the farm.

reached Red Cottage; but, being isolated, they were overcome later in the morning, except a few small parties who effected a junction with the right of the 63rd Brigade further north. Owing to the intense machine-gun fire from Fricourt on any sign of movement in the open, it was not found possible to reinforce the survivors of the third and fourth companies in the German front trench, and they remained there until dark, the battalion losing 22 officers and 688 other ranks in the day's fighting.'

One of the most remarkable stories to emerge from these events was that of Lieutenant Philip Howe whose story is retold superbly in Martin Middlebrook's *The First Day on the Somme*. If you stand at the entrance to the German cemetery, north of Fricourt, looking west across the Contalmaison road, Lonely Trench, which was Howe's objective, is just a few yards beyond the other side of the road.

Following quickly behind the 10th West Yorks 'A' Company of the 7th Green Howards, commanded by Major Kent, had also attacked, at 7.45 am, south of the Tambour, in the direction of Fricourt Trench just north of Wing Corner. This attack was made erroneously and the men were annihilated by a single machine-gun within twenty yards of their own trench.

In the midst of the 1st July nightmare, the most terrible day ever experienced by the British Army amidst the unrelentingly dreadful casualty returns of the Great War, the 10th West Yorks suffered the highest number of casualties of any battalion engaged during any single day's action. After the attack Lieutenant Philip Howe could only muster approximately 40 men. Since the battalion had left some 170

Sassoon's view encompassed the site of the Tambour Mine craters and the British lines running northwards which faced the German trenches astride the Fricourt spur. On the horizon stand the two woods known as the Willow Patch and Round Wood. Central in the photograph is Fricourt New Military Cemetery. The British trenches can be seen clearly, running northwards from just to the left of the cemetery across the horizon to the left of the Willow Patch.

WILLOW PATCH

BRITISH FRONT LINE

FRICOURT NEW MILITARY CEMETERY

men behind on other duties, such as ammunition, water and ration carrying, stretcher bearers, QM staff, cooks, an HQ party and a battalion reserve, the casualty rate amongst the 750 men who actually took part in the attack was almost certainly in excess of 90%. However, the disaster experienced by the 10th West Yorks meant that the Subsidiary Attack on Fricourt, due later in the day, would take place without any protection on its northern flank where a number of German machine-gun teams in the Tambour area would wreak havoc.

The assault made on Mametz on the morning of 1st July (7th Division)

On the left of the 7th Division's front there was no attack from Wing Corner eastwards to Kiel Trench's junction with an important communication trench known as Shrine Alley. However, from Danube Trench eastwards the 7th Division attacked with five battalions in line abreast, the 2nd Borders, 9th Devons at Mansell Copse, 2nd Gordon Highlanders on the north side of the Peronne road, the 1st South Staffs facing Bulgar Point and the 22nd Manchesters on the right boundary of the division. In this frontage four Russian saps had been driven forward to positions close to the German front line and these were opened shortly after zero giving considerable protection to subsequent movements across No Man's Land. Shrine Alley led back towards the village of Mametz, which was surrounded by an important second line of defence, known as Orchard Alley on the west and Cemetery Trench to the south. In the south-western corner of the village one cellar housed machine gun teams firing through loop holes cut in four inch thick armour plated steel. Just south of Cemetery Trench was the small communal cemetery. Within the confines of the cemetery a shrine had been converted into another menacing machine-gun position. Officers of the 9th Devons understood all too well that their attacks to the north-west, across Danube Trench and Shrine Alley, would be enfiladed by this machine gun in the event of it not having been put out of action by the preliminary bombardment.

Behind 20 Brigade's assault battalions the supports were arranged as follows. The 8th Devons, 2nd Royal Warwicks and 2nd Royal Irish were echeloned back through Ludgate Circus and Lucknow Redoubt. Behind the 91st Brigade the 2nd Queens supported the 22nd Manchesters whilst the 21st Manchesters supported the attack of the 1st South Staffs. The right of the 7th Division's assault lay north of Minden Post, to which Geoffrey Malins was driving, having filmed the detonation of the mine at Hawthorn Ridge near to Beaumont Hamel at

Private Jack Stead, 1598, 10th West Yorks, Killed in Action in front of Fricourt on 1st July 1916. Private Stead carried this card, which also shows his wife Harriet and daughter Mary, into battle. The card was recovered after his death. On the reverse one of his friends has written, 'This chap was one of my pals. I found him dead on the [battle]field.' On the outbreak of war Private Stead had enlisted into the Bradford Pals and the reason why he was with the 10th West Yorks is not known. Jack Stead is buried in the New Military cemetery at Fricourt. [Swift]

7.20 am. At Minden Post Malins's purpose would be to film the activity behind the front lines. This morning he was joined by another cameraman, Macdowell, who was intent on filming the wounded who would begin to pass through this position after the first attacks.

On the left of that part of the 7th Division's frontage from which an assault was to be made at 7.30 am, four small mines, in the area of Kiel Trench, were detonated at 7.28 am. The whole area at the southern end of Shrine Alley and its junction with Kiel Trench and Danube Trench was already peppered with craters across which an attack would have been difficult since the uneven ground hid many saps and hollows ideally sited for defence. The attack of 20 Brigade was therefore very exposed on its left since the small mines did not destroy the German positions in that area. I have already mentioned the concerns which many harboured about the likely impact of the machine-guns south of Mametz in the area of the communal cemetery and Shrine Alley. When 20 Brigade's assault began the 2nd Borders moved forward towards their objective at Apple Alley, which would be 20 Brigade's inner defensive flank. After crossing Danube Support Trench the 2nd Borders moved to their left whilst coming under direct machine-gun fire from Mametz as well as Fricourt. However the Borders pressed on, now enfiladed from their right by machine-gun fire coming from Hidden Wood. By 9.30 am the southern part of Hidden Lane was taken by the 2nd Borders and Hidden Wood was then cleared of German troops by an attack across the open, combined with a bombing raid down the portion of Hidden Lane which ran into the wood. Soon afterwards the Border's men entered Apple Alley, thus securing their objectives. However, there was at this stage in the morning no battalion on the Border's right flank and therefore the Subsidiary Attack planned on Fricourt, which took place at 2.30 pm, was not adequately protected on its right flank.

East of the Borders, in the area of Mansell Copse, the attack of the 9th Devons was marked by disastrous casualties. Because of the difficulties of exiting from Mansell Copse, the 9th Devon's attack was launched from support trenches some way to the rear of the front line. Nevertheless, the danger of the machine-gun at the Shrine had been accurately predicted by Captain D.L.Martin. Inevitably the 9th Devons were caught as they left their trench in the field south of the copse.[16] The men were forced to file slowly through and around the copse in front of their trench and were cut down before they could make any significant progress. Immediately a gap opened between the 9th Devons and the 2nd Gordons to their right and only very small numbers of the 9th Devons managed to get across No Man's Land over the German front line Danube Trench, after which they consolidated within Tirpitz Trench. The 8th Devons were rather more fortunate in crossing Danube Trench and entering Shrine Alley. In the afternoon

1st July 1916. The 7th Division's men at Mametz.

these units were joined by two companies of the 2nd Warwicks from divisional reserve and they were able to cross Shrine Alley after a bombardment of those positions at 3.30 pm, thereafter bombing forward along Danzig Trench, crossing Rose Trench and finally taking up position at their objective, in Orchard Alley and Orchard Trench west of Mametz village, by late evening. During this period of the fighting some two hundred German prisoners were taken from the area of southern Mametz and around the Shrine. By late afternoon the Borders were in their objectives on the extreme left of 20 Brigade's attack with parties of the 8th Devons to their right in Orchard Alley Trench. By 4.05 pm the area north of Mametz, including Bunny Trench, had been gained.[17]

On the right of the Devons, north of the Peronne road, stood the 2nd Gordon Highlanders. This battalion was tasked with attacking towards The Halt, at F.11.a.0,3, a small station on the Albert - Peronne light railway line which passed to the south of Fricourt and Mametz. Such an attack meant that they were facing directly towards the Shrine past which they would have to move before capturing the western end of

Mametz.[18] The Gordons were handicapped in that their left flank was immediately left unprotected by the disastrous circumstances which overtook the 9th Devons. The men nevertheless advanced with incredible bravery in the face of overwhelmingly heavy fire. Remnants of this attack forced their way forward, initially reaching Shrine Alley south-east of the communal cemetery. Later, with the support of the 8th Devons they advanced to take part of Cemetery Trench, the remnants of the battalion reaching that part of Bunny Trench west of Mametz by 4.00 pm.

To the right of 20 Brigade's attack 91 Brigade proved to be far more successful. As their attack developed the first battalion to fight their way into Mametz was the 1st South Staffs. The South Staffs' advance had been aided by the two mines exploded under German saps on Bulgar Trench. The larger of the mines was set under Bulgar Point, on the battalion's right flank. During the first few minutes the South Staffs were met by heavy shrapnel and machine-gun fire. Moving steadily forward they took a considerable number of prisoners before being held up on the southern outskirts of the village at Cemetery Trench, which these men reached by 7.45 am.

By 8.00 am the 22nd Manchesters were in Bucket Trench, east of

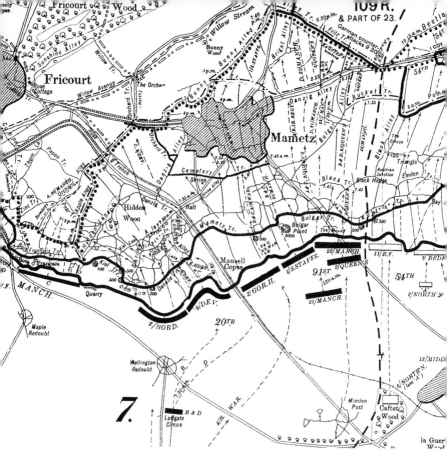

Map 6. Detail from the disposition map showing the position of the 7th Division's units south of Mametz at zero hour on 1st July.

Mametz, and the first of the South Staffs' men were into the outskirts of Mametz. However, at this stage it was not possible to progress further because of the intensity of the rifle and machine-gun fire from Danzig Alley and Bunny Trench north of the village. The 7th Division's narrative of these events says that,

> 'during these operations casualties were very heavy and two companies 21st Manchester Regiment were sent up in support. On the right a counter-attack from Fritz Trench drove the 22nd Bn Manchester Regt out of Dantzig Alley. It was therefore impossible to launch the 2nd Bn Queen's Regt to their objective. This battalion had occupied a position of readiness in our old front line when the assaulting troops moved to the attack. The General Officer Commanding 91st Infantry Brigade at once ordered one company 21st Bn Manchester Regt to support the 22nd Bn Manchester Regt in an attack on Dantzig Alley, so as to

enable the 2nd Bn Queen's Regt to advance through Fritz Trench to their final objective, the necessary artillery barrage having been arranged.'[19]

A re-bombardment of Danzig Alley, Fritz Trench and Bunny Alley was ordered, but this also failed to produce the conditions in which the men could advance. A further bombardment at 12.45 pm, allied to the fact that Pommiers Redoubt, to the right in XIII Corps' area, had fallen now meant that the advance of 91 Brigade could continue. Soon after 1.30 pm Danzig Alley east of Mametz was in the hands of the 22nd Manchesters and some men belonging to the regiment's 21st Battalion. On their left the 1st South Staffs, with two companies of the 21st Manchesters, now occupied that part of Danzig Alley running through Mametz. Bright Alley, north-east of Mametz leading towards the Queen's Nullah, was taken by bombers by 1.40 pm. However, at this stage a number of Germans were still resisting in other pockets of the wreckage north of the Montauban - Fricourt road which ran east to west through the middle of Mametz.

The 2.30 pm Subsidiary Attack on Fricourt

Some accounts of these events on the opening day of the Battles of the Somme have treated the frontal attacks upon Fricourt as if they

The site of Danube Trench, west of Mansell Copse. This segment of Danube Trench was assaulted by the 2nd Borders on the extreme left of the 7th Division's frontage during the main attack at 7.30 am on 1st July. The trench is clearly visible on the rising ground above the embankment which runs across the lower part of the photograph. Fricourt Wood can be seen to the right of the photograph. The stand of trees in the centre did not exist in 1914 but the tops of the trees forming Hidden Wood can just be made out on the horizon to the left of the central stand of trees. The pre-war track which ran directly to Bray-sur-Somme, from The Halt, south of Mametz, can be seen across the centre of the photograph where it cut Danube Trench at this point.

N WOOD

FRICOURT WOOD

were contiguous with the attacks made either side. That is not true. In the context of the 1st July the frontage allotted to the two battalions which were to undertake the Subsidiary Attack was exceptionally lengthy. However, the chances of success were anticipated as high, since the attack was to be delayed until such time as the flanks were secured, by the 10th West Yorks to the north of Fricourt and the 2nd Borders to the south-east of the village. It was true that, east of Fricourt, the attacks by XV Corps at Mametz were progressing slowly and those by XIII Corps past Pommiers Redoubt had succeeded greatly. Unfortunately, from the area of III Corps, to the north of Fricourt, Lieutenant General H.S. Horne commanding XV Corps was being told, wildly optimistically, that British troops passing Peake Woods were moving on Contalmaison and that German artillery was being withdrawn from the Pozieres area. Horne therefore ordered the attack at 2.30 pm in the belief that the situation was more opportune than subsequent events proved it to have been. The Official History is rather critical of this situation.

'In view of this encouraging outlook, and because the preliminary bombardment of the Fricourt sector seemed to have been very successful, General Horne decided to order the initiation of the third phase of the battle, the attack up the Willow Stream valley on Fricourt and Fricourt Wood. As a matter of fact the units attacking on either side of these localities had not yet reached the whole of their first objectives or had even formed, except partially on the right, any defensive flank towards Fricourt. Moreover, the second phase, the advance beyond Mametz and Fricourt Farm towards the German second intermediate line covering Mametz Wood, had not yet been begun. .... But orders were received (by units involved in the

This panorama shows the site of the 9th Devons' attack across Danube Trench towards Shrine Alley. Mametz communal cemetery and the site of The Shrine can be seen clearly, just below the church. On the right of the photograph is Mansell Copse, where many of the men killed during this attack are now buried in their old front line trench.

THE SHRINE

Subsidiary Attack) for the attack to proceed, that is Stage 2 was
to be carried out regardless of the failure of Stage 1.'[20]

Immediately to the west of Fricourt the early afternoon attack was
made by the 7th Green Howards, now effectively only three companies
strong after A Company's demise at 7.45 am. Their front line ran from
the communal cemetery, opposite Wing Corner, northwards to the
Tambour. On the Green Howard's right, south of Fricourt, the 20th
Manchesters had the longest frontage allotted to any battalion's attack
this day: from the communal cemetery opposite Wing Corner along the
length of Aeroplane Trench, facing Sunken Road Trench, to the quarry
east of Bois Francais (F.10.c.8,3) and south of the Bois Allemand area.
They would attack with the assistance of two companies of the 2nd
Royal Welsh Fusiliers as well as the RWF's bombers.

Without dwelling at too great a length on these events it was
predictable that they would not go well. Private Pat Burke serving with
the 20th Manchesters wrote that,

'All those weary hours the lads remained calm, but very eager
to get it over. They did not go over after a strong ration of rum as
some people imagine these affairs are carried out, no, they went
over feeling themselves. The Colonel watched them mount the
steps, and his last words were, "Isn't it wonderful." The way they
extended to six paces, and walked over at the slope one would
have thought they were at Belton Park or our other training
quarters. Our reserves were calling out "Bravo Manchesters"
"Good Luck" "Cheer Oh" and every word of praise that such
calmness could bring to their minds. Down they fell one by one,
but no excitement occurred until they closed on the German
front line....' *(Private Pat Burke, in a letter written on 7/7/1916.)*

Siegfried Sassoon, still well placed in Kingston Road Trench to
witness this attack, confirms the impression of an almost unconcerned
optimism which seemed to pervade the Manchesters' ranks.

'2.30. Manchesters left New Trench and apparently took
Sunken Road Trench, bearing rather to the right. Could see about
400. Many walked casually across with sloped arms. There were

MANSELL COPSE

The view towards The Halt from the Gordons cemetery showing the direction of their attack on the morning of 1st July 1916. On the left of the photograph is Mansell Copse and the Albert to Peronne road. After the war The Halt (or station) was rebuilt on the same site and still stands today (1997).

about 40 casualties on the left (from machine-gun in Fricourt). Through my glasses I could see one man moving his left arm up and down as he lay on his side; his face was a crimson patch. Others lay still in the sunlight while the swarm of figures disappeared over the hill. Fricourt was a cloud of pinkish smoke. Lively machine-gun fire on the far side of the hill. At 2.50 no one to be seen in No Man's Land except the casualties about half way across. ....'

As Sassoon witnessed, the bulk of the first waves of the 20th Manchesters crossed without too many casualties. But on the left, near to Wing Corner, the Manchesters' detachments due to bomb down towards Fricourt along Kitchen Trench and Copper Trench were almost wiped out.

Sassoon's notebook entry at 5.00 pm says,

The German perspective. Looking towards the site of the attack, made by the 9th Devons and the 2nd Borders, from The Shrine in the main German support trench south of Mametz.

MANSELL COPSE

FRICOURT VILLAGE   MAMETZ VILLAGE

The scene of the attacks towards Mametz, made by the 1st South Staffs moving from the left of this photograph, west of The Mound, towards the village church, on the horizon just left of the road. Fricourt is visible in the very centre of the photograph. On the extreme left of the photograph is Mansell Copse, on the slopes above the Albert to Peronne road. Bois Francais is behind the prominent stand of trees on the left horizon. The 22nd Manchesters attacked diagonally across the line of the road heading towards the eastern end of Mametz, beyond the far right of the photograph.

'I saw about thirty of our A Company crawl across to Sunken Road from New Trench. Germans put a few big shells on the Cemetery and traversed Kingston Road with machine-gun. Manchester wounded still out there. Remainder of A Company went across - about 100 altogether. Manchesters reported held up in Bois Francais Support. Their colonel went across and was killed.'[21]

The RWF's bombers were able to bomb up Sunken Lane Trench both towards Fricourt for a while and towards The Rectangle, east of Aeroplane Trench. Some Manchesters briefly got into The Rectangle and bombing duels were later fought as attempts were made to get eastwards along Orchard Alley. However, by nightfall there had been very little progress other than to occupy Sunken Road Trench, south of Wing Corner, and the German support trench north of Bois Francais[22].

Between Wing Corner and the German Tambour positions the attack made by the 7th Green Howards had been disastrous. This battalion's assault had been strengthened by the bringing up of the 7th East Yorks who were moved into the front lines west of Fricourt, C and D Companies occupying the trenches from which the ill fated attack by the 10th West Yorks had been made that morning, and A and B in immediate support of the 7th Green Howards. When orders were received from XV Corps detailing the 2.30 pm attack, 50 Brigade had signalled that it was pointless to carry this out west of Fricourt in view of the failure of the morning's attack to establish a defensive flank to their left. The brigade was overruled. Before the attack there had been a short artillery bombardment, but it had signally failed to damage the wire or threaten the deep dug-outs. When the Green Howards attacked at 2.30 pm, their three companies faced the strongest part of the

Fricourt defences either side of Wicket Corner and immediately came under intense machine-gun fire, from positions to their front and also from the Tambour on their left. Germans were seen standing on their own parapets to fire. Within 180 seconds the 7th Green Howards' casualties were over 350 men and officers. One small group got into the village but were all killed or captured apart from a few soldiers who took shelter in a ruined cellar where they stayed overnight. North of the Green Howards the 7th East Yorks had also attacked, on their commanding officer's own initiative, three minutes later. Again the casualties were overwhelming and no men of the 7th East Yorks were able to cross No Man's Land north of the Tambour.

The afternoon of 1st July, at Mametz and north of Fricourt

Following the re-bombardment of the Mametz area at 3.30 pm, the combined weight of the Warwicks, Devons, South Staffs, Gordons and 21st Manchesters had forced their way through to the northern side of the village, Fritz Trench and Bunny Trench having been taken by 4.00 pm. By 5.00 pm all was quiet in the village. By 6.30 the 2nd Queen's had taken all of Fritz Trench and Bright Alley east and north of the village. As evening drew on the South Staffs then moved up Bunny Alley to link up with the Queen's, thus securing the entirety of Mametz village and the 7th Division's objectives there. Mametz was placed under the command of Lieutenant Colonel Norman of the 21st Manchesters; the whole of the new frontage of the 7th Division was wired that night; wells were cleared and supply dumps established and a wireless station was set up in the south western part of the village. Unfortunately, in pursuit of unnecessary security, a great opportunity had been missed since German resistance on the whole frontage from east of Fricourt to beyond Montauban seemed to have broken down.

However, the situation north of Fricourt unfolded less satisfactorily for the 21st Division's men in that location. It had been hoped that the 2.30 pm Subsidiary Attack on Fricourt would allow 63 Brigade to advance to and capture Fricourt Farm (Ferme du Bois) which lay half a mile north-east of the village, whilst 64 Brigade's men, further to the north, would capture Shelter Wood. In 63 Brigade's area the machine-gun fire from Fricourt Farm and Fricourt Wood proved far too strong. North of Lozenge Wood 64 Brigade were already at their first objectives, Crucifix Trench, and had attempted attacks on Shelter Wood at 1.40 pm, after which they had repelled a series of German counter attacks at 2.00 pm. Thereafter 64 Brigade's position did not change and orders were issued to arrange for their relief by the 12th

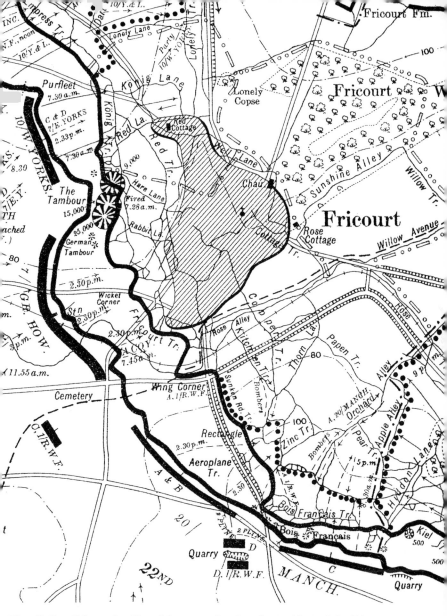

Map 7. Detail from the disposition map showing the position of the 7th Green Howards and the 20th Manchesters who were involved in the Subsidiary Attack on Fricourt at 2.30 pm on 1st July 1916.

and 13th Northumberland Fusiliers. By dawn of the 2nd July, 64 Brigade's men were forming a defensive flank facing the north of Fricourt. The casualties amongst 64 Brigade's men had been the heaviest of all the brigades engaged at Fricourt and Mametz on 1st

July.[23] However, by dusk on the 1st July it was apparent to 50 Brigade that the Germans opposite were weakening and beginning to withdraw. Arrangements were set in hand for the two remaining companies of the 7th East Yorks alongside the 6th Dorsets to attack the now relatively weakly held village. However, these orders were overruled by the 21st Division's CO, Major General Campbell, and arrangements were put in hand to relieve 50 Brigade by 51 Brigade. Congestion meant that this relief was not completed until 5.00 am of 2nd July.

On the 7th Division's frontage, north of Mametz, General Watts recorded that,

> 'Patrols were sent forward during the night July 1st/2nd by the 22nd Bn Manchester Regt to Queen's Nullah which they found unoccupied; and by the 1st Royal Welsh Fusiliers with orders to bomb as far as Wing Corner; also by the 2nd Royal Irish Regt into Fricourt, which they reported clear.'[24]

But the chance to occupy Fricourt quickly was not taken and it was not until midday on the 2nd July that British troops belonging to the 17th Division from Corps' Reserve were able to advance through the village. Looking back with the benefit of hindsight, it seems unfortunate that where success had been achieved as part of a general

Private Pat Burke, nearest to camera, with other soldiers belonging to the 20th Manchesters, the 5th City Battalion. Pat Burke was killed in the Ypres area during 1917.

AEROPLANE TRENCH   TAMBOUR CRATERS

The site of the assault made by the 20th Manchesters, part of the Subsidiary Attack at 2.30 pm on 1st July. This photograph was taken a few yards to the west of Bois Francais proper where D Company of the 20th Manchesters and D Company of the 1st RWF were assembled prior to their attacks. The British front line, Aeroplane Trench, ran across the field facing the village of Fricourt. To help orientate the photograph the Tambour craters are central whilst the Willow Patch lies on the horizon, centre right.

attack, whose avowed intent was to facilitate a speedy advance deep into German held positions, the response of the corps' command here at Fricourt in bringing the reserve troops forward was so hesitant.

Lieutenant Bernard Adams later died of wounds, at Serre, on 27th February 1917. He was buried at Couin Military Cemetery.
Bernard Adams. *Nothing of Importance.* pp 163.
'Schloss Fricourt' or Fricourt Chateau was located on the north-eastern side of the village, amongst the trees of Fricourt Wood, the right as you enter the lane leading north towards Fricourt Farm. After the war the Chateau was rebuilt on the left side of road.
Oldham Battalion of Comrades: Book of Honour. Pub. Sherratt and Hughes. Manchester 1920.
The soldiers named in Adams' book have had their true identities hidden by the use of imaginary names.
Manchester Pals. Stedman. Pub Leo Cooper. 1994.
The 24th Manchesters had converted to Pioneer Battalion status on 22nd May 1916.
The northern mine, located at F.3.a.4,3, was 9,000 lbs. The central mine at F.3.a.4,0 was 15,000 lbs whilst the southern largest e, located at F.3.c.4,8, was 25,000 lbs.
Although the Tambour mines are still very visible, in fact well preserved under their canopy of trees and undergrowth, the es in the vicinity of Kiel, Danube and Bulgar trenches have been progressively filled during the intervening years and are onger easily found unless you are equipped with an adequate map.
Official History. Military Operations, France and Belgium, 1916. Vol 1. pp 348.
Official History. Military Operations, France and Belgium, 1915. Vol 11. pp 300-335.
Lynch and Haswell are buried almost side by side in Plot I, Row B of Norfolk Cemetery.
Official History. Military Operations, France and Belgium, 1916. Vol 1. pp 356.
Official History. Military Operations, France and Belgium, 1916. Vol 1. Appendices 23 (i & ii). pp 184-190 inclusive.
Of the other COs in 64 Brigade, Lt Col C.W.D. Lynch, 9th KOYLI, was already killed, Lt Col M.B. Stow, 1st East Yorks had n mortally wounded and Lt Col H.J. King wounded. Captain Gordon Haswell of the 9th KOYLI, whose toast had saved the osphere at the last meal before the battle, was killed. In all 24 KOYLI officers became casualties on 1st July 1916.
The Devonshire cemetery now occupies part of the original British front line trench south of Mansell Copse at F.11.c.5,3.
king from the location of the cemetery, the direction of the 9th Devon's attack lay towards the north-west and not in the ction of Mametz itself.
The 2nd Border's casualties were 334 men and officers.
Many first time visitors to Mansell Copse and the Gordons cemetery believe that the Gordons were attacking due north, rds the east of Mametz, from their positions adjacent to the Peronne road. Such an interpretation is mistaken. As with the Devons the direction of the Gordons attack was to the north-west in the direction of The Halt along the course of the Albert ronne road and light railway.
PRO. WO95/1631.
Official History. Military Operations, France and Belgium, 1916. Vol 1. pp 362-3.
Lieutenant Colonel H.Lewis.
There is a far fuller account of the actions involving the 20th, 21st and 22nd Manchesters at Fricourt and Mametz in chester Pals, Stedman, pub Leo Cooper.
Casualties in XV Corps' area exceeded eight thousand men and officers, 3,380 in the 7th Division, 4,256 in the 21st Division 1,155 in 50 Brigade of the 17th Division. In the corps' area 29 German officers and 1,596 other ranks had been made prisoner ar.
PRO. WO95/1631.

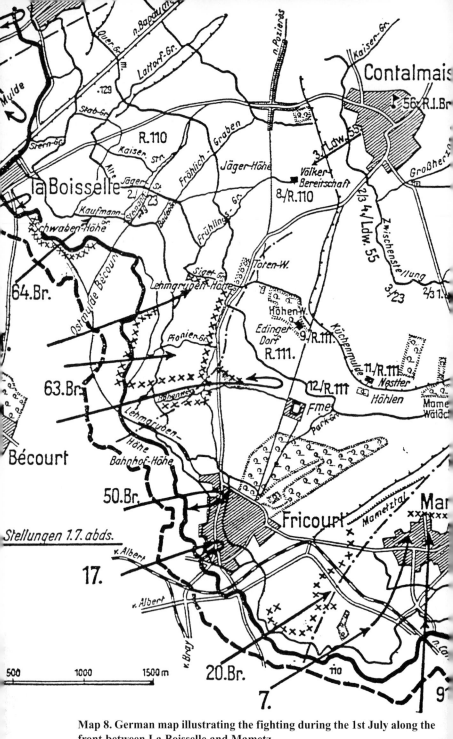

Map 8. German map illustrating the fighting during the 1st July along the front between La Boisselle and Mametz.

Chapter Three

FURTHER EVENTS IN THE AREA OF FRICOURT AND MAMETZ DURING THE SUMMER OF 1916

The Rear Areas south of Fricourt and Albert

Before describing the events which occurred immediately after 1st July's fighting it is worth considering the vital role played by the railways which lay behind the front lines, as well as villages and locations involved in the quartermastering, supply and medical evacuation of the British troops engaged in the Battle of the Somme. The area covered by this guide included the most important of the Fourth Army's supply facilities. The main British railhead in the area was at Dernancourt junction, on the Amiens to Arras main Nord line (see map page 74). Dernancourt was ideal in that the village is surrounded by a large expanse of open ground in the valley of the Ancre. From Dernancourt a double track military standard gauge line led towards the mass of sidings maintained at Meaulte, then south towards Pilla Junction and then eastwards along the Plateau Line as a single track past Grovetown in the direction of Happy Valley and The Loop. This line linked, at the site of the Loop, with a single metre gauge line which then ran north, in the direction of Fricourt, past the Citadel, and south towards Bray-sur-Somme. However the majority of

This informative photograph shows the employment of German Prisoners of War in the transfer of wounded stretcher cases from an ambulance to a Hospital Train at Dernancourt, September 1916. Two wounded men are already placed on the ground behind the German soldiers.

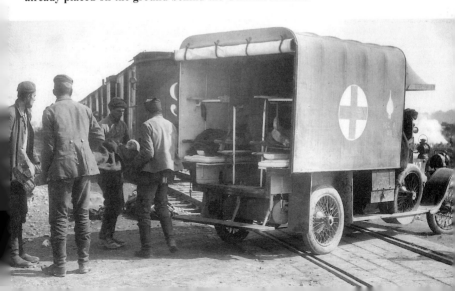

This photograph shows one of the 12 inch rail mounted guns firing from a position in the Ancre valley somewhere between Meaulte and Dernancourt during August 1916.

the ammunition was sent forward from Dernancourt on lorries or horse drawn wagons. After the first week's fighting, and the relative success of the British efforts in the vicinity of Montauban and Mametz, it became apparent that the greatest emphasis would be placed on the southern sector of the battlefield. Therefore, the supply arrangements which led north from the Loop, through Fricourt and past Mametz Wood, were to become central in the logistics of the battle as they were extended to cope with the vastly increased levels of traffic which was routed through these locations. Throughout this period ambulance trains used the Dernancourt - Loop line and both the communal and extension cemeteries in Dernancourt contain the graves of many men who died whilst in the caring hands of Field Ambulances, Casualty Clearing Stations and Main Dressing Stations in that vicinity.

En route for The Loop the trains passed through the village of Meaulte, which lies on the Albert to Morlancourt road. Meaulte was, even by 1916's extraordinary standards, a very distinctive place. Not only was it occupied by British troops but also by roughly 75% of its pre-war population, who were reluctant to move even though they were being subjected to occasional shelling. There seemed to have been little love lost between the two groups and the villagers had a nasty reputation for profiteering shamelessly. There was a large encampment nearby, at a location known as the Sand Pit, at E.18.d.3,3, where many units bivouacked before going up the line. The village's billets were regarded as being amongst the most filthy and squalid that the men who used them ever recalled. By late spring of 1916 there were many railway sidings south-west of the village. Later, as the fighting moved eastwards, the extensive railway facilities here at Meaulte were expanded with the construction of the Meaulte - Martinpuich line running north-eastwards through Becordel, Becourt, Fricourt, along the Willow Stream valley past Bottom Wood and up towards Bazentin and Longueval. By that time the military and capital investment in this area was huge, there being at least 35 sidings for the storage and movement of locomotives and wagons in the Meaulte - Vivier Mill area by the end of November 1916. To get the locomotives up onto the higher ground south of the battlefield the line ran south-west from Meaulte junction following close to the present day course of the D42 before swinging east, around the spur north and above Morlancourt, along what was known as The Plateau Line leading towards Happy Valley and The Loop. Incidentally, just east of Morlancourt was the railway junction known as Pilla Junction from which a French operated branch went to their railhead known as Bel Air!

By contrast, Morlancourt lies on the road between Albert and the village of Sailly-Laurette on the banks of the River Somme. Although Morlancourt was not vital to the British supply effort, many French troops passed through en route for the fighting to the south east. However, the village was well known to many soldiers who served within the 7th Division and who were often billeted here in the spring of 1916. Graves, Sassoon and Adams, serving with the 1st Royal Welsh Fusiliers, knew the village well and their books mentioned it frequently. After a spell in the front line and immediate support positions the battalions would march out through Meaulte and thence by a circuitous route of six miles into what was regarded as the very cosy spot of Morlancourt. Such a roundabout route was designed to

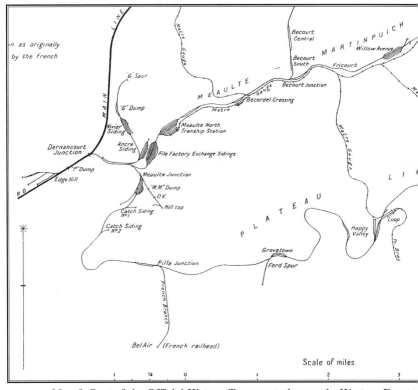

Map 9. Part of the Official History, Transportation on the Western Front - Map number 5, dealing with British railway lines on the Somme.

ease traffic congestion on the Fricourt to Bray road but must have been terribly hard on the soldier's feet after days in wet trenches. Morlancourt village was sufficiently far to the west to be out of artillery range and the billets here were deemed clean, dry and comfortable. On still evenings it was, however, still possible to hear the tapping of the machine-guns at the front line and see the glare of the flares. Bernard Adams wrote of how, 'it thrills like the turning up of the footlights.' But Morlancourt was no rest place. When out of the lines the soldiers billeted here were taken for working parties on the railway lines and sidings being constructed in the Meaulte - Bray - Loop triangle.

The other village closely linked with the fighting at Fricourt and Mametz is Becordel-Becourt. This village lay roughly a mile and half south-west of Fricourt, in the direction of Meaulte, on the Albert to Peronne light railway line. Because of its proximity to the front lines this whole area had been utterly smashed by shelling, even before the 1st July's battle began. Any vestiges of woodland were utilised to disguise ration stores and artillery dumps. There were many deep shelters for troops in the locality, dug beneath any cellars and embankments. The road from Albert, running past the site of the Albert French National Cemetery, was the main route for motorised and horse drawn transport. At the start of the Battle of the Somme the 14th Field Ambulance was here in Becordel-Becourt. XV Corps, commanding the divisions at Fricourt and Mametz, had a walking wounded post here as well as an Advanced Dressing Station.

Some miles to the east of Morlancourt lay Happy Valley, just off the Bray - Fricourt road. This was the site of a huge encampment where thousands of men stayed, both before and after their part in the battles. The valley was where reserve units of the Fourth Army were rested and held in reserve. Happy Valley is located a little way south-west of the Citadel on the southern limits of trench map sheet 62.d.NE2 in squares F26 and 27 as well as L2 and L3. As the battle progressed in July and August exhausted soldiers bivouacking here still found sleep impossible because the northern part of the valley was used by many artillery units, occupying terraces of gun pits in the position known as Gibraltar (F.26.d.). By late summer the earth was parched and bare, all of the blackening trees were clearly witnessing a last summer, dying because the animals had gnawed away at their bark. Many French units passed through this area and the surrounding roads were always congested with French and British horse drawn transport. The air was inevitably dust laden and valuable supplies of water had to be brought up on carts from the River Somme at Bray because the dry chalk of Happy Valley harboured no natural water supply for the soldiers or the thousands of pack horses and mules which were constantly being led down to troughs to drink. Units which found the time then sent their men down to the Somme to clean and refresh themselves in its water. A few yards to the west of the valley ran the Albert to Bray road which was always busy with military traffic. Here, on higher ground west of Happy Valley adjacent to the railway lines running from Dernancourt, was another tented encampment known as Fork Tree camp. Apart from its thousands of transient soldiers, the Happy Valley area provided hutted accommodation for medical teams, wheelwrights and repair craftsmen, sanitary units and the military police. Many diarists and observers spoke of this valley as being like a vast market place, with worn out divisions resting briefly being sent on to quieter areas and new units in bivouacs pondering the trial they were soon to undergo.

BRONFAY FARM

THE LOOP

The site of The Loop, photographed from the Bray - Mametz lane. The narrow gauge railway line ran into the field opposite and turned in a huge sweep in order to lose height before travelling down the valley, southwards, in the direction of Bray. On the left horizon is Bronfay Farm.

Throughout all there were brief opportunities for friends and the simply inquisitive to ask how things were going. Almost invariably the answers were that it had been like hell.[1]

Incidentally, yet another camp for men entering the arena of battle was located in the Bois des Tailles, south-west of Happy Valley, astride the Morlancourt to Bray road. Before the fighting on 1st July many soldiers from both the 7th and 21st Divisions spent time in the Bois des Tailles, being rotated out of the front lines to enable them to carry out training as well as providing working fatigues on the construction and maintenance of the railways, in the area north of Bray towards the Loop and the Citadel. In late May Siegfried Sassoon described the wood as being full of men from the Devon and Border battalions within the 7th Division, following men from the 21st Division who had been there earlier in the month. Shelter from the elements, a good distance from the anxiety of the front, and the proximity of the River Somme made this a far more popular encampment than those in the Happy Valley area. Only the ever present crashing clamour of the artillery's guns breached the peace here!

North of Happy Valley the railway skirted the artillery's positions at Gibraltar before crossing the Bray - Fricourt road and entering the Loop which is still very visible today. On your IGN map the Loop's area is denoted as 'le Fer a Cheval' which translates as 'the horseshoe'. It can be reached on foot along the line of the overhead cables running eastwards from the D147 road just south of Chataigneraie Farm, south of Citadel New Military Cemetery. Walk along the line of the cables until you meet the lane running north from Bray in the direction of Mametz. From here you look out across the site of The Loop. During the spring and early summer of 1916 The Loop provided a rail terminus from which huge quantities of supplies were taken northwards, initially by mule and carrying parties but later, as the fighting extended away from Fricourt and Mametz, by metre gauge railway line. The atmosphere here was one of intense activity as materials and some munitions were passed on to forward units. The Loop can be located on sheet 62.d.NE2 in the vicinity of square F28 central.

2nd July at Fricourt and Mametz

Overnight the position in front of Fricourt village was quiet. Behind the German front lines the soldiers of 111th RIR began to withdraw at about 11.45 pm. At the British XV Corps HQ orders were issued for a 75 minute bombardment at 11.00 on the morning of the 2nd, to be followed by an attack by 51 Brigade at 12.15 pm[2]. However, as we have already seen a patrol mounted by the 2nd Royal Irish of the 7th Division entered Fricourt from the direction of Mametz unopposed at midnight and later, soon after dawn, patrols of the 8th South Staffs collected over 100 prisoners of the 111th RIR. But the story is one of seeming lethargy and is well told by the Official History, which shows how these events unfolded.

'There were so few signs of resistance that at 8.50 am Major General Pilcher [commanding the 17th Division] directed the 51st Brigade to advance into the village without waiting for the bombardment; but the changing of orders caused considerable delay, and Fricourt was not entered until noon. There was no fighting, and only eleven German stragglers were rounded up.'

North of the village the forward movement of British troops within 51 Brigade continued past the Chateau and across Fricourt Wood, behind a protective barrage, with the objective of reaching Bottom Wood. In order to visualise these events it is easy to walk north from the German Military Cemetery at Fricourt, turning right along the first lane, leading to Fricourt Farm (Ferme du Bois on your IGN map), from where these events can be clearly seen in context.

On the left of 51 Brigade, which was facing the south-west aspect of Fricourt Farm, patrols from 10th Green Howards, 62 Brigade, 21st Division, pressed towards the farm from the north of Lozenge Wood (the trees on the left of the lane leading to Fricourt Farm). Roughly 75

Bombardment of Fricourt on the 2nd of July TAYLOR LIBRARY

prisoners and two machine-guns were captured by these patrols. By early afternoon the 10th Green Howards had moved forward close to The Poodles, which were 100 metres north of the farm astride the track leading into Shelter Wood (Bois de Fricourt Ouest)[3]. Meanwhile the 7th Lincolns passed through the confines of Fricourt Wood but were unable to progress further towards Bottom Wood. After that success the position north of Fricourt remained static until, at 11.00 pm, east of the Poodles and roughly 300 metres north of Fricourt Wood, part of Crucifix Trench and Railway Alley were secured by a bombing attack made by the 10th Sherwood Foresters.

By the end of the day the 7th Lincolns, the 8th South Staffs and the 10th Sherwood Foresters of 51 Brigade were in control of the area north-east and east of Fricourt from The Poodles, where they were adjacent to the 10th Green Howards' men of the 21st Division, along the fragment of Crucifix and Railway Alley to the north of Fricourt Farm. Their positions then ran along the north and eastern limits of

Bombardment of Fricourt. A quote from the back of this photograph written at the time reads, *'From this very spot the British offensive was launched 1st July 1916, thus starting that terrrible and wretched battle of the Somme. I spent a miserable night in the fields directly in front of this battery in July, but I did not slumber.'* TAYLOR LIBRARY

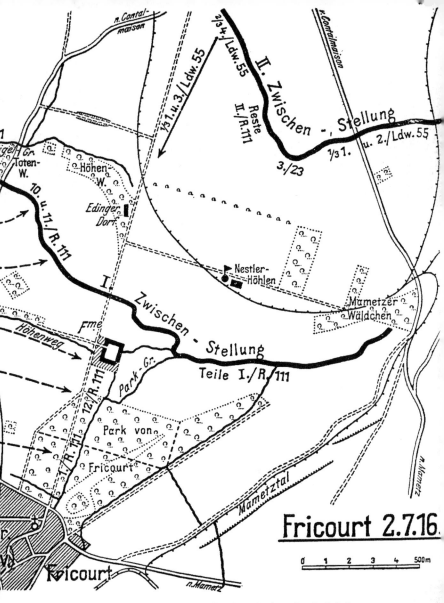

Map 10. German map illustrating the fighting during the 2nd July at Fricourt.

Fricourt Wood and thence down Willow Trench and Orchard Trench until coming into contact with the men of the 8th Devons, of the 7th Division, who had consolidated on the Mametz - Fricourt road the previous evening.

Overnight on 1st/2nd July it had been similarly quiet at Mametz. By

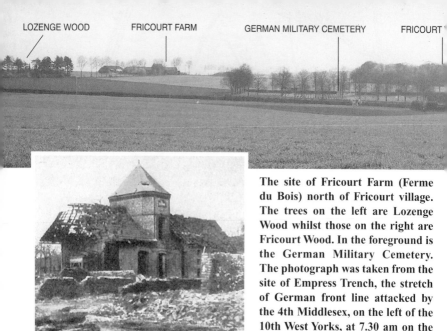

LOZENGE WOOD   FRICOURT FARM   GERMAN MILITARY CEMETERY   FRICOURT

The site of Fricourt Farm (Ferme du Bois) north of Fricourt village. The trees on the left are Lozenge Wood whilst those on the right are Fricourt Wood. In the foreground is the German Military Cemetery. The photograph was taken from the site of Empress Trench, the stretch of German front line attacked by the 4th Middlesex, on the left of the 10th West Yorks, at 7.30 am on the 1st July 1916. By the close of 2nd July's fighting this area had been captured and was under the control of 51 Brigade.

On left Fricourt farm before the battle.

dawn it was realised that the ground to the north of the village was free of German soldiers. Accordingly at 7.30 am 91 Brigade were ordered to occupy Queen's Nullah and the western portion of White Trench, which lay one kilometre north east of Mametz facing the southern flank of Mametz Wood. Access to this area from Mametz is simple by following the unclassified Contalmaison road from the north of

A view of Fricourt, captured on the 2nd July by the British. TAYLOR LIBRARY

Mametz. After 750 metres Queen's Nullah is to your right. Just north of Queen's Nullah the road forks and if you care to take the right fork White Trench can be found on the slightly elevated ground on the right of the road 600 metres after the fork. From here you can get a very clear view of the southern approaches to Mametz Wood. By 11.00 am the 2nd Queen's were in possession of this area, having captured a small number of prisoners together with one machine-gun. South east of Fricourt the soldiers of 22 Brigade were able to advance across Kitchen, Pearl and Papen trenches towards Rose Trench, which ran alongside the Albert - Peronne light railway, from their positions north and north-west of Bois Francais.

Early in the afternoon Siegfried Sassoon was still able to view these events from his vantage point at Kingston Road Trench, just above the communal cemetery. His notebook recorded that,

'2.30 pm. I am now lying out in front of our trench in the long grass, basking in sunshine where yesterday there were bullets. Our new front-line on the hill is being shelled. Fricourt is full of troops wandering about in search of souvenirs. The village was a ruin and is now a dust heap. A Forward Observation Officer has just been along here with a German helmet in his hand. Said Fricourt is full of dead; he saw one officer lying across a smashed machine-gun with his head bashed in - 'a fine looking chap' he said, with some emotion, which rather surprised me.'

Thus, by the end of 2nd July, the first line of objectives set for the 21st Division on the 1st July had been captured, north of Fricourt Farm. Almost all of the objectives set for the Subsidiary Attack on Fricourt had been captured, whilst the 7th Division had reached their second objectives and a significant proportion of their third objectives. However, north-east of Fricourt village Bottom Wood, which should have been captured by the convergence there of the 7th and 21st

A panoramic view of Mametz. TAYLOR LIBRARY

Division's soldiers the previous day, still stood uncaptured. Similarly the main German Second Position, consisting of Quadrangle Trench and Wood Trench guarding the approaches to Mametz Wood, was still unshaken. Again, rather than focusing on the need to press forward the emphasis was placed on defence, the remainder of 2nd July being spent in ensuring that, as the Official History puts it, 'the whole of the line was consolidated and strongly wired.'

The failure to capture Mametz Wood on 3rd and 4th July

On the morning of 3rd July, starting at 9.00 am, XV Corps' troops made considerable progress in their fight for the area north-east of Fricourt in the approaches to Mametz Wood. East of Fricourt Farm the 7th Borders advanced under heavy fire in order to capture Railway Alley. Other units of 51 Brigade including the 7th Lincolns, 8th South Staffs and the 10th Sherwood Foresters were all drawn into this fighting. By 11.30 am Railway Alley was occupied, and some of the Borders' men even entered Bottom Wood, north of Mametz across the Willow Stream's valley. However the Borders were denied the pleasure of completing the capture of Bottom Wood by the 21st Manchesters, who had been able to enter the wood from the eastern end without recourse to fighting, capturing three field guns in the process. The

The ruined church in the village of Mametz pictured soon after its capture by the British. TAYLOR LIBRARY

initial approaches to Mametz Wood were now secured and two batteries of XIV Brigade RHA, were brought up into a very advanced position within Queen's Nullah to begin the process of cutting the wire in front of Quadrangle Trench and Wood Trench which protected Mametz Wood.

Simultaneously that morning the 21st Division's men captured Shelter Wood and Birch Tree Wood, north of Fricourt Farm. This was achieved by the 1st Lincolns together with the 12th and 13th Northumberland Fusiliers from support and reserve. The initial advance was undertaken by the Lincolns under the protection of fire from many machine guns. At first the men could not get beyond the perimeter of Shelter Wood, although stubborn resistance in Birch Tree Wood was overcome as the 12th Northumberland Fusiliers moved up

British troops line the steps of a dug-out, in Danzig Alley, which has survived the British bombardment. Probably photographed during the period 2-4th July 1916.

from support. At this point the Germans mounted a strong counter attack from within Shelter Wood and German reserves were seen from the air, moving forwards from Contalmaison. The 13th Northumberlands were then deployed from reserve and Shelter Wood was finally captured in the early afternoon. At 2.00pm a further German counter attack was launched against Shelter Wood and Bottom Wood, but this was again repulsed by the effective use of Lewis Guns. Later that afternoon the woods were scoured for stragglers and many prisoners were taken, 600 officers and men of the 186th Regiment were captured, together with 200 of the 23rd Regiment and the 109th, 110th and 111th Reserve Infantry Regiments.

However, this day also proved to be one of lost opportunity. Patrols undertaken at 3.00 pm revealed that Quadrangle Trench and Mametz Wood were empty. Two hours later, at 5.00 pm, XV Corps' commanding officer, Lieutenant General Horne, ordered that Strip Trench, Wood Trench and the eastern end of Quadrangle Trench be occupied, but only after dark. 22 Brigade were ordered to undertake this attack, moving forward from their concentration positions between Caftet Wood and Mansell Copse, deploying the 2nd Royal Irish and 1st RWF. Unfortunately these troops were let down by poor guiding and they were not in position to advance until the following morning. Overnight there was some patrol activity within Mametz Wood and it soon became clear that Wood Trench and Quadrangle Trench were held, albeit only weakly.

Siegfried Sassoon's account of these events describes how, earlier in the day, he left the sanctuary of his vantage point at Kingston Trench,

The view towards Contalmaison from Danzig Alley, east of Mametz. In the foreground is the Willow Stream valley and the eastern end of Bottom Wood which was captured by the 21st Manchesters. The small stand of trees beyond is Quadrangle Wood, above which the communal cemetery outside Contalmaison can be seen.

BOTTOM WOOD   CONTALMAISON   QUADRANGLE WOOD

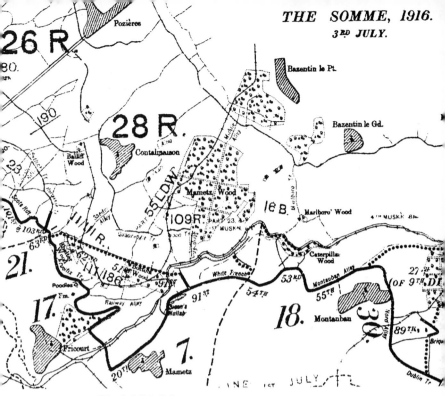

THE SOMME, 1916.
3RD JULY.

Map 11. Mametz Wood, 3/4th July.

from where he had overlooked the fighting for Fricourt, joining his battalion, the 1st Royal Welsh Fusiliers, and then the whole brigade at their concentration point between Caftet Wood and Mansell Copse. This was still the morning of 3rd July and rumours were soon circulating amongst the men, NCOs and subalterns that an attack on 'some wood' was imminent. Here the battalion rested until evening when orders came to 'dig a trench somewhere in front of Mametz'(Wood). As the men moved off Sassoon saw, 'arranged by the roadside, about 50 of the British dead. Many of them were Gordon Highlanders. There were Devons and South Staffordshires among them, but they were beyond regimental rivalry now...'[4]

Sassoon knew that the delays were dangerous and felt uneasy that, after four hours they had progressed no more than 1,500 yards into the outskirts of Mametz where the men were issued with RE equipment, picks, shovels, pickets and wire. The battalion's commanding officer 'was somewhere ahead of us with a guide. The guide, having presumably lost his way, was having a much hotter time than we were.' Later, in the pitch dark of 2.00 am, on the morning of the 4th July, the battalion's progress speeded up and the columns exited from the north

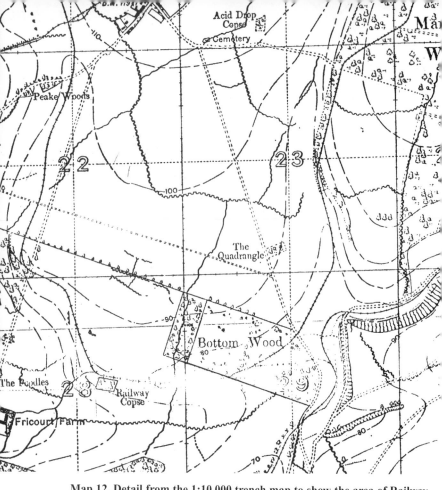

Map 12. Detail from the 1:10,000 trench map to show the area of Railway Alley, Bottom Wood, Queen's Nullah and the approaches to Mametz Wood.

of the village and entered a communication trench. Here the reality of the war was brought home as a number of recently killed German

This panorama shows the area within which 22 Brigade were concentrated during the morning of 3rd July, in the valley between Mansell Copse and Caffet Wood. On the right of the photograph is Carnoy whilst on the horizon lies Montauban, captured by the 30th Division during the first phase of the attack on 1st July 1916.

MONTAUBAN

soldiers lay about in fixed contorted postures.

'It gave me a bit of a shock when I saw, in the glimmer of daybreak, a dumpy, baggy-trousered man lying half sideways with one elbow up as if defending his lolling head; the face was gray and waxen, with a stiff little moustache; he looked like a ghastly doll, grotesque and undignified. Beside him was a scorched and mutilated figure, whose contorted attitude revealed bristly cheeks, a grinning blood-smeared mouth and clenched teeth.'

It was soon afterwards, when the 1st Royal Welsh filed out of this communication trench, that they realised the strength with which the Germans now held Mametz Wood. In front of Sassoon's battalion the Irish were taking casualties and the Welsh withdrew without firing a roll of barbed wire in anger! As Sassoon so sarcastically put it, 'It was obvious now that a few strong patrols could have clarified the situation more economically than 1,000 men with picks and shovels.'

The Official History of the Somme Battle apportions blame for the missed opportunities of 3rd July to the leadership of XV Corps, Lieutenant General Horne, stating clearly that:

'It would appear that if the XV Corps had encouraged more vigorous action on the afternoon of the 3rd, a hold on Mametz Wood could have been secured, and Wood Trench and Quadrangle Trench occupied. The last-named objective was taken on the morning of the 5th, but the others were to cost many lives and much precious time.'

The 4th - 10th July. The fighting for the approaches to Mametz Wood

On the night of the 3/4th July the 21st Division, which had initially attacked north of Fricourt on the morning of 1st July, was withdrawn to rest. The divisional artillery, however, remained active. The 21st Division's frontage was taken over by 52 Brigade, of the 17th Division. During the period 30th June to midnight of 3rd July the 21st Division suffered 4,663 casualties amongst its officers and men.

The following night, the 4/5th July, XV Corps planned a surprise night-time attack to capture the southern projection of Mametz Wood, as well as Wood Trench and Quadrangle Trench as far as its junction

CARNOY

MANSELL COPSE

MAMETZ VILLAGE

The route into Mametz, followed by 22 Brigade as they moved slowly forward on the evening of 3rd July to make their abortive attack on Mametz Wood's approaches, and where Sassoon saw many of the Gordons', Devons' and South Staffordshires' dead.

with Shelter Alley. The attacks on Mametz Wood and Wood Trench fall outside the scope of this guide, but those attacks against Quadrangle Trench can be dealt with here. The scene of these attacks can be visited by travelling along the Mametz to Contalmaison road until you reach the site of Bottom Wood. Today the shape of Bottom Wood is very much changed from its 1914 outline. However, standing in the foot of

Gordon Highlanders out to rest. Mametz Wood 1916. TAYLOR LIBRARY

the Willow Stream valley next to Bottom Wood (Vallee St Antoine on your IGN map) the locations of Wood Trench and Quadrangle Trench can be distinguished clearly to the north of your present location. During the 4th July much rain had fallen and the assault battalions' progress towards the front was hampered by mud and terrible congestion. The attack against Wood Trench was made by the 2nd Royal Irish with the 1st Royal Welsh Fusiliers on their left. On the left of the Welsh the 9th Northumberland Fusiliers and 10th Lancashire Fusiliers made the attack on Quadrangle Trench. Much of the credit for the success achieved by these two battalions can be ascribed to their having crept up to within 100 yards of the German position before zero hour, 12.45 am on the morning of the 5th July. These two battalions then charged forward, capturing Quadrangle Trench and Shelter Alley, taking prisoners from the 163rd and 190th Regiments. Unfortunately the attacks by the 2nd Royal Irish on the right were driven back, leaving the southern projection of Mametz Wood and Wood Trench uncaptured. That night the 7th Division was relieved by the 38th Division. Between 1st and 5th July the 7th Division suffered 3,824 casualties amongst its officers and men.

These events mark the beginning of the final phases of the 1916 fighting covered by this guide. Soon the emphasis would switch to the attempts being made by the 38th Division to capture Mametz Wood. However, before that process could proceed the trenches known as Quadrangle Support and Pearl Alley to its west and north-west had to be captured. The area between the western boundaries of Mametz Wood and Contalmaison communal cemetery, south-east of Contalmaison village, lies on the very north-eastern limits of this guide's area. I have therefore drawn upon a small section of text from the La Boiselle guide in order to help clarify the nature of the fighting in this area west of Mametz Wood.[5] By 7th July a period of strength sapping and devastatingly wet weather set in, making any effort almost intolerable for the men. As on the 4th, the weather during 7th July 1916 had a catastrophic effect on the trenches. The Official History reports that,

'The trenches became knee-deep, in some cases waist-deep, in clinging slime, and, under shellfire, collapsed beyond recognition. Movement was often an agony: men fainted from sheer exhaustion whilst struggling through deep mud; in some localities a team of fourteen horses was required to bring up a single ammunition wagon. Under such handicaps, the advance of reinforcements and the circulation of orders suffered grave

Looking westwards from the northern embankment of Queen's Nullah, photographed in 1997, Fricourt Farm can be seen in the distance on the horizon, with Fricourt Wood to the left. It was here at Queen's Nullah that Major General Ingouville-Williams, commanding the 34th Division, was killed later in July 1916.

> delay; and on many occasions artillery barrages were called for in vain, so frequently did hostile bombardments cut telephone lines in the forward areas where there had been no time to bury them.'

These were the sort of conditions which popular memory has associated with Passchendaele in the autumn and early winter of late 1917, yet this was the Somme in mid-summer 1916! I have concentrated upon the events which the 12th Manchesters endured at this time. This battalion was to play a significant part in the attacks upon Quadrangle Support and Pearl Alley, both trenches lying in the valley between Contalmaison and Mametz Wood. XV Corps was of the opinion that if these two trenches were captured the subsequent fight for both Mametz Wood and Contalmaison would be made easier. The memorial, erected to the memory of the 12th Manchesters' men, to be found at the back of Contalmaison's communal cemetery is a fine vantage point from which to visualise these events.

The 12th Manchesters were part of 52 Brigade of the 17th (Northern) Division.[6] This brigade had, as we have already seen, moved up to take over positions north of Fricourt in the late evening of 3rd July. That night the sunken lane leaving Fricourt towards Contalmaison was terribly congested with troops and it was fortunate that the

The south-western approaches to Mametz Wood. Central lies Bottom Wood with Mametz Wood on the extreme right of the photograph.

The 38th (Welsh) Division's memorial overlooking the southern approaches to Mametz Wood.

German artillery was not aware of the five battalions crowded onto this short stretch of track. This moment was, as we have already seen, one of the great missed opportunities of the Somme battle in that British patrols had found both Mametz Wood and Quadrangle Trench empty that afternoon. This extraordinary situation did not last for long and subsequent attacks on Mametz Wood and Quadrangle Trench, which lay between the southern tip of Mametz Wood and Contalmaison, became necessary. As we have already seen these attacks did improve the British position, although Mametz Wood still held. During those attacks on the night of 4/5th July the 10th Lancashire Fusiliers and the 9th Northumberland Fusiliers, took and consolidated Quadrangle Trench, although the attack against Wood Trench which was made by the 2nd Royal Irish with the 1st Royal Welsh Fusiliers on their left was less successful.

The plan of attack on Quadrangle Support, and Pearl Alley beyond, which the 17th Division was then ordered to follow by Lieutenant-General Horne was, at best, seriously flawed. Major-General Pilcher of 17th Division complained that even if these trenches were taken they could never be held whilst under the cross fire of machine guns in Mametz Wood and the vicinity of Contalmaison. Nevertheless, at 2.00 am in the complete darkness of the early morning of 7th July, following a 35 minute bombardment, fired rather inaccurately on map co-ordinates, the 10th Lancashire Fusiliers and 9th Northumberland Fusiliers attempted a further advance in order to capture Quadrangle Support. Those bleak early morning hours were marked by torrential

The view towards Mametz Wood past the site of the 12th Manchesters' memorial within Contalmaison's communal cemetery.

rain-showers and the attack was destined to fail, although some members of the Lancashire Fusiliers did manage to penetrate as far as Pearl Alley and the wreckage of Contalmaison. However, they were driven out by a determined counter attack by the Lehr Regiment and bombers of the 9th Grenadiers.

Later, the Corps' order for a renewed attack was only received by the 17th Division at 5.25 am, but telephone links forward of Brigade HQs were utterly unreliable. Consequently it was only at about 7.00 am that the 12th Manchesters were called up from their reserve trenches, further back on the Fricourt - Contalmaison road. As a result it was more than six hours after the initial and failed assault by the two battalions of Fusiliers, at approximately 8.03 am, that the 12th Manchesters and two companies of the 9th Duke of Wellingtons advanced towards Acid Drop Copse, the site of which is clearly visible just yards to the east, from the battalion's memorial, and Quadrangle Support Trench, in clear daylight under a now cloudless sky. The artillery bombardment which preceded this attack had still produced no discernible damage to Quadrangle Support Trench or its wire and to make matters worse the communication difficulties forward of Brigade headquarters had ensured that the men's assault was a few minutes late.

The view looking south-west towards Shelter Wood and Fricourt from the road opposite the Contalmaison communal cemetery. On the extreme right is Peake Woods cemetery.

PEAKE WOODS CEMETF

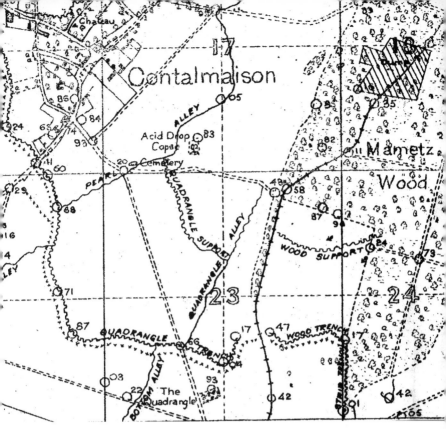

Map 13. Part of an original trench map showing the scene of the attacks made by the 12th Manchesters on the morning of 7th July 1916. Quadrangle Support is the trench which initially runs parallel to the track between Contalmaison communal cemetery and the wood shown as The Quadrangle, which lies between Bottom Wood and Mametz Wood.

Having formed up behind the hedge running west from Bottom Wood the 12th Manchesters had attacked across Quadrangle Trench, still occupied by the other battalions of 52 Brigade. The delays meant that the Manchester soldiers lost any protection from their own barrage, which had now shifted forward, leaving the German troops who were defending Quadrangle Support able to deliver a withering rifle fire in the face of the attackers. 52 Brigade's objective was 700 metres distant and as soon as the men showed themselves on the higher ground overlooking Quadrangle Support they were devastated by severe machine gun fire, mostly coming from Mametz Wood on the right, suffering 16 officer casualties and 539 amongst the men. The few survivors were later brought back under the supervision of their commanding officer, Lieutenant Colonel E.G.Harrison. A few posts remained out and they were engaged all day long in skirmishes with enemy bombing parties. Only two officers remained unwounded. Major-General Pilcher's concerns had come, terribly and fully, to realisation.

However, there is nothing to be gained from further narrative detailing the fighting west of Mametz Wood and south-east of Contalmaison. It is nevertheless worth noting that the area around, Contalmaison communal cemetery, where the 12th Manchesters' memorial was erected after the war, does provide fine viewing, both towards Mametz Wood to the east and towards Shelter Wood, Crucifix Trench and Fricourt towards the south-west. The cemetery was the site of a German trench, known as the Grossherzog, which ran through the cemetery from Quadrangle trench to the south-west. Grossherzog then exited the rear of the cemetery, near to the 12th Manchesters' memorial, and ran eastwards into Quadrangle Support and Acid Drop Copse. There is some evidence that the site of the original, pre-war, cemetery was located a few yards to the left of the present day cemetery and that the bulk of the graves contained therein were destroyed by shellfire during the 1916 fighting.

1. The track leading into the valley north of Bray Vale Cemetery on the Bray to Albert road is the easiest point of access into Happy Valley.

2. On Sunday 2nd July weather was again good, temperature 75° F,although the morning was overcast. On 3rd July the temperature was 68° F, fine, with some cloud and thunderstorms to the south-east. On 4th July the temperature was 70° F, overcast with thunderstorms.

3. The Poodles, 100 metres north of Fricourt Farm, was a small cluster of trees located at 57.d.SE4. X.28.a.3,1. It is worth noting that the shape of Shelter Wood has altered considerably since the Great War, before and during which there were no trees on the eastern side of the track running north from Fricourt Farm.

4. Siegfried Sassoon. *Memoirs of an Infantry Officer.* The location described by Sassoon is almost certainly the site of the Gordons Cemetery below Mansell Copse.

5. For a fuller description of the fighting within the approaches to Mametz Wood see the guide to that place which forms a further volume in this series.

6. 52 Brigade consisted of.
        9th Northumberland Fusiliers.
        10th Lancashire Fusiliers.
        9th Duke of Wellingtons.
        12th Manchesters.

Chapter four

THE YEAR OF 1918

So many of the cemeteries within the area covered by this guide contain the graves of soldiers killed during the final eleven months of the war that it is impossible to avoid dealing, albeit very briefly, with the fighting which took place during 1918. I have included within Chapter Six a brief tour and guide to these events which should help you follow the story's outline. One rather chastening fact which reveals itself all too clearly in the cemeteries which relate to the August 1918 fighting is the high proportion of very young soldiers who were killed at this time. These were the Men of 18 of 1918 and their sacrifice is especially notable in Ville-sur-Ancre communal and military extension, Morlancourt British Cemetery Number 2, together with Bray Hill and Bray Vale cemeteries. Meaulte Military cemetery also contains a number of these pitifully youthful soldiers killed as the war began to ebb away in the severe fighting which characterised the late summer and autumn of 1918.

During the spring of 1918 the German Army had planned a last desperate effort to gain advantage before the impact of the Allied blockade and the arrival of American troops swung the battlefield balance against the Kaiser's troops. Albert came to have a prominence in these events, as it did in so many others which figured in the

German troops in the vicinity of Bray-sur-Somme, 1918.

GERMAN ADVANCE BY DAYS
March 1918.

REFERENCE.

Zero		————
22nd March (morning)		2
23rd " "		3
24th " "		4
25th " "		5
26th " "		6
27th " "		7
28th " "		8
29th " "		9
5th April (final position)		●●●●

Map 14. The German advance by days. March 1918. Opposite page 533. OH. 1918 Vol 1.

extraordinary history of the Great War. The outcome of the German spring offensive was a considerable advance which left the British clinging to positions west and south-west of Albert in a desperate attempt to prevent the German Army capturing the vital town of Amiens. The town of Albert was captured by the Germans on 26th March 1918. Thus, between the 21st March and 29th March the retreat across the Somme battlefield from St. Quentin, past Peronne to Albert had cost the British Army a thirty mile width of territory, but the change in the balance of morale and spirit had swung very much in favour of the unbeaten British units. The Official History puts the situation in context.

'Whilst the enemy's physical exertions were perceptibly weakening, his morale was failing, as was shown by the increasing numbers of small surrenders and by the changed attitude of the prisoners, arrogant on the 21st and 22nd March, confident of victory on the succeeding days, and now on the 26th bewailing the loss of their comrades, and, at heart, indifferent to the outcome of the battle. In the great majority of the British units, on the other hand, morale had actually improved. The junior officers and N.C.O.'s had begun to feel conscious that they had emerged from their ordeal unbeaten in spirit and still ready to fight; they had learned much in a few days of open warfare,

British guns in the square of Albert in 1917, before the German offensive on 26th March 1918. TAYLOR LIBRARY

The remains of Albert railway station after the 1918 fighting when the town practically became No-Mans-Land. TAYLOR LIBRARY

and were better prepared for further fighting of this nature; the constant change to new scenes had refreshed their efforts, and, above all, the decrease in artillery fire had relieved the strain on their nerves, always severely tried in the constant and accurate bombardments of trench warfare.' [1]

The German's somewhat Pyrrhic success thus left the British Army on the western side of Albert, having lost Mametz and Fricourt but more significantly having lost the railhead facilities which were concentrated at Meaulte and Dernancourt. Morlancourt was also lost, leaving the village of Ville-sur-Ancre as the British front line village south-west of Albert. The German Army had therefore established itself on high ground once more, that east of Morlancourt being especially valuable in that it gave observational control over both the Somme and Ancre river valleys.

The late spring and summer months then became a period of time in which the British Army prepared itself for the huge effort which would ultimately win the war against Germany. The German army's spring initiative had failed to divide the British and French armies. Whilst the German military machine was exhausted and suffering a progressive decline in its preparedness and morale the British Army was infused with thousands of eighteen and nineteen year old conscripts. The area covered by this guide then saw some of the fighting which was encompassed by two of the most significant battles of late 1918, the Battle of Amiens and the Second Battle of Albert.

On 8th August 1918 the spring-time roles were reversed, following a massive onslaught on the German army undertaken by both the British and French armies. The French effort, to the south of the Amiens–Roye road, was known as the Battle of Montdidier. The British focus of this onslaught, the Battle of Amiens, was the two roads running east and south-east from Amiens where the attack was undertaken by the Australian and Canadian Corps under the command of the Fourth Army. The village of Ville-sur-Ancre was at the very northern-most limit of that attack and in this area the British 12th Division was engaged in the attack. Some progress was made that day towards Morlancourt and Sailly-Laurette, on the River Somme to the south, was re-captured. The following day, the 9th August, Morlancourt and Dernancourt were re-captured as the Fourth Army continued to press forward towards Etinehem and Bray, just north of the River Somme, using the British 58th and the 3rd and 4th Australian

The almost complete destruction of Albert Basilica, during the 1918 fighting. TAYLOR LIBRARY

Whippet Tank.

Divisions south of the river. By 11th August Etinehem had been taken and the British Fourth Army stood in positions overlooking Bray, although Albert had, as yet, not been subjected to any attempt to re-capture it. These events therefore left the German Army in control of a salient which included Albert on its north-western flank and Bray-sur-Somme at its southern-most limit.

The Second Battle of Albert, again fought by the troops of Rawlinson's Fourth Army, began on the heavily misted morning of 21st August. Later that day the weather became clear and hot. Similar conditions prevailed on the 22nd and on the 23rd the weather created 'a day of great heat'. I have given some detail, below, of the fighting which followed on during these hot summer days because the terrain should be familiar to those of you who have studied the area south of the Albert - Fricourt road. The main attack on 22nd August, undertaken by III Corps, involved an advance of approximately two miles across a

Map 15. Detail from a 1:20,000 map showing the area of the Citadel, Happy Valley, The Loop and Bray-sur-Somme with trenches corrected to 3/8/1918. Note the extensive railway facilities which had been constructed in this area before the German advance of March 1918.

four mile frontage. By contrast with the meagre gains which were occasionally made during the 1916 campaigning in this area, the contemplation of an advance of two miles in a day seems quite remarkable. The advance was timed to start at 4.49 am, with nothing more than four minutes of preparatory artillery fire to enable the men to assemble behind the protective curtain of shellfire. The fighting for control of the low ground between Meaulte and Albert was a task given to the men of the 18th Division ensuring that Bellevue Farm and Vivier Mill were re-captured. South of the River Ancre the fighting for Meaulte and the ridge leading across to the locations north of Happy

101

Valley was undertaken by the 12th Division's men. South of the 12th Division the 47th (2nd London) Division were given the task of capturing the Bois des Tailles and the Happy Valley area. This advance would take the men past the grim sight of a large 1916 burial ground, now Grove Town cemetery, which had been established by the 34th and 2/2nd London Casualty Clearing Station on the higher ground of this ridge west of Happy Valley. The extreme right of this attack would be covered by the 3rd Australian Division.

These events would see extensive use made of tanks. Ten Mark V's of IV Tank Brigade were allotted to the 12th and 47th Divisions, whilst the 18th Division was allotted four tanks. Arrangements were also made to ensure that, if the objectives east of Becourt and Happy Valley were captured, cavalry and Whippet Tanks would be available to seize the high ground between Bois Francais (Sheet 62. D. NE. 2. F.10.c.) and Great Bear Copse (F.22.d.)

The artillery arrangements showed how much the tactics of this arm had evolved during the preceding three years. In the frontage allotted to the 12th and 47th Divisions the men would follow a creeping barrage, advancing at the rate of 100 yards every four minutes until the final objective was met. In order to make the barrage line absolutely clear, to the many youthful and inexperienced troops, smoke shells were to be included in the proportion of 1:15 shells fired.

To add to the growing evolution of tactics a great deal of bombing was undertaken from the air. Because the night of 21/22nd August was fine and clear navigation was straightforward. More than twelve tons of bombs were dropped on Cambrai railway station; the sheds at Marcoing station were damaged and the railway bridge at Aubigny-au-Bac was hit. Bombers also struck at the aerodromes at Moislaines and Offoy. The intention was to disrupt the German ability to bring reinforcements forward and to cause chaos in their communications network.

However, during the night of 21/22nd the German Army fired a succession of harassing barrages using 4.5" high explosive shells and gas shells. At 2.30 it opened a barrage of the British lines and used machine-guns to continuous effect. When the British barrage opened at 4.45 am on another misty morning there was an immediate retaliation response on the batteries.

Nevertheless, the attack made by the 3rd Australian Division achieved its objectives, advancing to the valley north of Bray, just south of the site of Bray Vale Military cemetery and consolidating there by 8.15 am. Bray itself was not attacked since it was strongly held

DIRECTION OF HUSSARS' ATTACK

The view looking up Happy Valley which was the scene of the 1/1st Northumberland Hussars' abortive attack on the morning of 22nd August 1918.

and could be better dealt with once a secure hold had been gained on the high ground to the north, which overlooked the small town. However, the 47th (2nd London) Division rather fell short of achieving its objectives. The Official History noted that 141 Brigade of the 47th Division had a difficult task.

> 'Owing to bad staff work and the insufficient training of the young troops in movements in darkness, smoke, and mist, the two leading battalions, 1/20th and 1/19th London, lost count of distance and though the Germans surrendered freely, the battalions halted considerably short of the intermediate objective, as much as half a mile short on the right.' [2]

142 Brigade following behind had an even more difficult task on its hands and was met by determined resistance. On 142 Brigade's right the 1/22nd Londons got to the southern end of Happy Valley, where Bray Vale cemetery stands today, but the other battalions were unable to get forward in the face of German artillery being fired over open sights from the ground above the eastern confines of Happy Valley, that is from positions south of Chataigneraie Farm and along the Fricourt - Bray road towards Bray Hill cemetery. Only one of the tanks allotted to 142 Brigade got as far as Happy Valley, which it entered and then succeeded in rounding up a number of German prisoners before having to be withdrawn because of crew casualties and engine trouble. Happy Valley then became the scene of a disastrous situation which allowed the 1/1st Northumberland Hussars to ride forward east of Happy Valley without knowledge of what would face them in the vicinity of the Bray - Fricourt road. The Whippet Tanks had already broken down when two squadrons of the Hussars entered Happy Valley from its southern end and headed for the high ground to the north east, which in fact was still in German hands. As soon as the leading

103

squadron topped the rise they were met by close range rifle and machine-gun fire as well as bombing from the air! With just 23 men left the squadron rallied under the shelter of the embankments in the Albert - Bray road west of the southern end of Happy Valley where they were joined by the second squadron. Although these unfortunate and inappropriately used mounted soldiers were then withdrawn, the 47th Division's men had no difficulty consolidating their gains across the high ground west of Happy Valley and this day's operations north-west of Bray were therefore concluded by 8.00 am.

North of the 47th Division's men the 12th (Eastern) Division was able to take Meaulte, this time somewhat assisted by the effects of the mist which enabled small detachments of soldiers to take many positions by surprise. In the town of Albert the 18th Division's men had been instructed to form a defensive flank to protect the northern-most limits of the advance expected to be made by the British 12th and 47th and Australian 3rd Divisions already mentioned. Between Albert and Meaulte the advance across the Ancre was undertaken by 54 Brigade, whose patrols overnight managed to position a number of trestle bridges to enable the marshy, shell shattered river course to be crossed. By 4.45 am 16 foot bridges spanned the Ancre and by 8.00 am 54 Brigade's men were past Bellevue Farm and consolidating their gains. North of 54 Brigade the town of Albert itself was cleared by the 8th East Surreys, who took advantage of the mist to surprise many of the German's posts on the strongly held east side of the town. The advance should have then been continued by the 7th Buffs but, such was the

Cinematic camera team going up to film. TAYLOR LIBRARY

Meaulte village. 23rd August 1918. The same camera team at work.

intensity of fire from the western slopes of Tara Hill, no further
advance could be made beyond the eastern limits of the town's
wreckage.

During the afternoon of 22nd August there were various attempts by
the Germans to disrupt the advanced forces of the 47th Division. To
some extent these succeeded in pushing some units of 142 Brigade
back until they rejoined the soldiers of 141 Brigade in what had been
the intermediate objectives of the day's advance. Nevertheless, the
Fourth Army had obliterated the German salient on the ridge east of
Morlancourt and had re-captured Albert and the important railheads to
the south.

On the morning of 23rd August various operations drove the
German Army further from Albert. These were undertaken by the 18th
Division working in conjunction with the 38th (Welsh) Division. The
38th were north of the Albert to Bapaume road and attacked at 4.45 am
towards the Usna Hill, crossing that and securing their objectives.
Meanwhile the 18th Division were only able to progress some 1000

yards east of Albert and were left below the summit of Tara Hill. Some progress was also made on the banks of the Somme towards the south of Bray-sur-Somme by soldiers of the 3rd Australian Division. This day the 47th and 12th Division's men were not engaged in fighting.

By the early morning of 24th August Bray-sur-Somme had been secured by the 3rd Australian Division's men. The attacks this day had been launched at 1.00 am in bright moonlight. However, as the morning unfolded, the weather became cloudy and cooler, drizzle setting in until, by midday, low cloud and poor visibility made all arms co-operation with the RAF difficult. Nevertheless, Becordel and Becourt villages and Becourt Wood also fell to the soldiers of the 18th Division. During this day the 12th and 47th Divisions were also re-engaged. The area around Happy Valley and the higher ground on the ridge south-east of Meaulte then saw heavy fighting involving both the 12th and 47th as well as the 58th Divisions, some of whose troops were used from reserve. Although more than 300 German prisoners were captured within Happy Valley by soldiers of the 1/15th London (47th Div.) the high ground near to Grove Town cemetery was the scene of intense fighting after a gap appeared between the 12th and 47th Divisions at this location during the early morning's advance. The cause of this problem was two strong points being manned by soldiers of the German 115th Regiment of the 25th Division. Their machine guns caused havoc amongst the men of the 6th Royal West Kents and 6th Queen's as well as the 21st Londons. Three tanks from the 1st Tank Battalion were deployed in order to clear up the situation, but their attempts failed, two being disabled and the third tank's guns jamming. It was not until 6.00 pm that the ground north-west of Grove Town cemetery was captured, by which time the positions of Becordel-Becourt and Happy Valley were secure.

During the subsequent two days the remains of Fricourt and

Grove Town Cemetery, looking across the plateau towards the Bois des Tailles.

A view of a street in Albert photographed just as the Germans had been pushed out. TAYLOR LIBRARY

Mametz villages were re-captured along with positions to the south of Fricourt including Bois Francais and The Citadel. This extraordinary success marked the establishment of conditions of more fluid open mobile warfare. After its success at Albert, the 18th Division soon found itself fighting across its old July 1916 battlefield, this time past Danzig Alley and Pommiers Redoubt towards Montauban from the west. Within days the Fourth Army's soldiers were overlooking Peronne, by 29th August, whilst the Third Army's soldiers captured Bapaume, on 30th August. Within ten days a huge area of territory had been crossed and made secure, including the entirety of the 1916 Somme battlefield, by a British Army making use of all-arms tactics capable of being followed by a nucleus of battle-hardened troops and the many youthful and inexperienced conscripts who now appeared in great numbers within every infantry unit. Thus it is true to say that Albert and the villages of Ville-sur-Somme, Dernancourt, Meaulte and soon after Fricourt and Mametz witnessed the rapid evolution of mobile warfare, right at the start of the last 'Hundred Days' of the Great War. Even as September days began to shorten it was clear that war had finally left these villages and the processes of re-occupation began. Initially the villages were the scene of battlefield clearance teams' work, but by the summer of 1919 the civilian population began to make their way home, commencing the process of transforming a devastated wasteland into that fertile source of sugar beet and other root crops which it had always been in the decades prior to 1914.

1. Military Operations in France and Belgium. 1918. Vol 1. pp 533.

2. Military Operations in France and Belgium. 1918. Vol 1V. pp 199.

The photograph below shows just one of the many perfectly maintained cemeteries in the Fricourt Mametz area. This scene was captured in Fricourt New Military Cemetery in the spring sunshine, 1997.

Chapter five

THE CEMETERIES AND MEMORIALS

In this Chapter I have grouped the cemeteries and memorials within the confines of an associated village. Those villages are:

† Bray-sur-Somme, including Bray Hill, Bray Vale and the Military Cemeteries within the town.
† Becordel-Becourt, including Dartmoor and Norfolk cemeteries. Dernancourt including the communal and communal extension cemeteries.
† Fricourt, including the New Military Cemetery, Bray Road, the two Point 110 cemeteries and the Citadel New Military cemetery.
† Mametz, including the Gordon, Devonshire and Dantzig Alley cemeteries.
† Meaulte, including Meaulte Military and Grove Town cemeteries.
† Morlancourt, including the No 1 and No 2 British cemeteries and Ville-sur-Ancre cemetery.

With so many cemeteries within one guide such an arrangement seems preferable to a strictly alphabetical format and should help those of you walking or touring the area to visit closely related cemeteries and memorials. I have given a brief introduction to the role played by the villages which lay behind the British lines in the supply and quartermastering of the British Army's effort in this area during 1916, at the start of Chapter 3.

The decision about which cemeteries to include was a difficult one. There are a number of other interesting cemeteries beyond the southern and western areas which form part of this guide. Some of these cemeteries contain the graves of men killed during the fighting which took place within this guide's area and I apologise if, on the grounds of available space, I have not included details of those cemeteries on the periphery such as Beacon Cemetery at Sailly Laurette as well as the cemeteries in the Chipilly and Etinehem area on the Somme south-west of Bray.

Here it is also worth noting that a considerable number of small cemeteries were created immediately after the fighting on the 1st and 2nd July in the Fricourt and Mametz area. Today a few of these still exist, for example the New Military Cemetery at Fricourt or the Gordons cemetery south of Mametz. However, a number of other cemeteries which were created at that time by battalion survivors have since been concentrated into the largest of the cemeteries in this area, Dantzig Alley east of Mametz. I have mentioned these cemeteries below in order to explain why some of the units engaged here on 1st July appear to have no representative cemetery of the kind created after similar experiences suffered by nearby battalions.

† **Aeroplane Trench cemetery, Fricourt.** This was the German front line south of that village. It contained the graves of 24 NCOs and men of the 20th Manchesters, the 5th City Battalion, who were killed attacking the trench on 1st July.

† **Bulgar Alley cemetery.** This was created in the German trench protecting the east of Mametz and contained 24 graves, all but one of which belonged to men of the 22nd Manchesters.

† **Hare Lane cemetery, Fricourt.** This was to the west of the village a few yards east of the Tambour mine craters and was named after a German communication trench there. It contained 54 graves of men who fell there on 1st and 2nd July, of whom 49 belonged to the 10th West Yorkshires.

† **Mansell Copse cemetery and Mansell Copse West cemetery.**[1] Mansell Copse cemetery was adjacent to the Devonshire cemetery but Mansell Copse West was some 500 yards distant in the vicinity of Danube Trench, attacked by the 2nd Borders on 1st July. These two cemeteries contained the graves of 51 soldiers who were killed, serving with the 2nd Borders, on 1st July 1916.

The usual criterion for maintaining a cemetery, used by the Commonwealth War Graves Commission, was numbers, forty being the usual minimum. However, problems with accessibility and relatively small numbers sometimes led to the concentration of possibly viable cemeteries into larger ones.

BECORDEL-BECOURT
Dartmoor Cemetery

This cemetery, then known as Becordel-Becourt Military Cemetery, was begun by British troops in August 1915. It lies just north of the village on the minor route to Becourt, very close to the D938 Albert - Peronne road. In May 1916 the cemetery's name was changed to Dartmoor at the request of the 8th and 9th Devons. The design of the cemetery maintains the distinctive touch brought by its designer,

Dartmoor Cemetery, Becordel-Becourt.

Edwin Lutyens, to many cemeteries and memorials on the Somme battlefield. In September 1916, towards the end of the Battle of the Somme, XV Corps maintained an Advanced Dressing Station here, next to the cemetery.

The cemetery contains a number of distinctive graves including that of Lieutenant Colonel Allardice, killed whilst commanding the 13th Northumberland Fusiliers on 1st July to the north of Fricourt and Lieutenant Henry Webber who was the oldest officer killed whilst serving with the British Army during the Great War, at 68 years of age. Before enlisting Webber had completed a career spanning more than forty years on the London Stock Exchange. He had succumbed to wounds, on 21st July 1916, received during the fighting at Mametz Wood. Also buried here are Sergeant George Lee and Corporal Robert Lee of A Battery, 156 Brigade RFA, a father and son who were killed on the same day, 5th September, 1916.

Soon after the war additional memorials were raised within the cemetery, firstly by the New Zealand Division to the memory of their men and officers who were killed near Flers in September and October 1916 and also by the 100th Machine Gun Company to record their losses during July 1916. These memorials have both since gone. The cemetery now contains the graves of 768 soldiers, only six of whom are unknown.

Norfolk Cemetery

This well known cemetery lies on the road between Becordel-Becourt and Becourt. Either side of the narrow valley within which the cemetery is situated are woods, those to the east being under the shelter of a relatively well protected reverse slope within which numerous gun pits were constructed. Until the 1960s this site often gave up many brass charge cases which the gunners had discarded in the area. Today it is more likely to reveal a harvest of refuse which is tipped in the vicinity of the small quarry south of the cemetery. At the top of the slope above the woods to the east of Norfolk Cemetery was Queen's Redoubt, 1000 yards east of the Tambour positions which faced Fricourt. This valley also marked the start of many important communication trenches such as Briton Street, Surrey Avenue and Queen's Avenue within which troops were moved to the front lines facing Fricourt. Running parallel to the road, by the side of the cemetery, was Middlesex Avenue trench and the first graves were dug adjacent to the site of that trench.

The cemetery contains the graves of many soldiers who served within units of the 21st Division. The cemetery was first used by the 1st Norfolks, after their arrival, in August 1915. Later the cemetery was expanded by other units including the 8th Norfolks until its closure in August 1916. After the war a considerable number of additional graves were concentrated here from outlying and isolated burial grounds, forming Row D of Plot I as well as Plot II either side of the Great Cross. The cemetery now contains 549 graves, amongst which 226 are those of unknown soldiers.

Perhaps the best known of the soldiers buried here is Major Stewart Walter Loudoun-Shand VC., 10th Yorkshire Regiment. *Officers Died in the Great War* describes Major Loudoun-Shand as having been killed in action during March 1917 but the cemetery register gives the date of death, correctly, as 1st July 1916. For some inexplicable reason the Official History gives no details of Loudoun-Shand's deeds on 1st July. However, during the night of 30th June his battalion had spent time at Queen's Redoubt, before being sent forward to support the attacks being made by 63 and 64 Brigades north of Fricourt. The

Norfolk Cemetery.

citation for his Victoria Cross, reported in the London Gazette on 8th September 1916, explained that,

Major Stewart Loudoun-Shand, 10th Green Howards. .

> 'When his company attempted to climb over the parapet to attack the enemy's trenches, they were met by very fierce machine-gun fire, which temporarily stopped their progress. Major Loudoun-Shand immediately leapt on the parapet, helped the men over it, and encouraged them in every way until he fell mortally wounded. Even then he insisted on being propped up in the trench, and went on encouraging the non commissioned officers and men until he died.'

Another senior figure of note, buried here in Norfolk cemetery, is Lieutenant Colonel Colmer Lynch, Commanding Officer of the 9th KOYLI, who had proved to be so unpopular with his fellow officers before the battle had begun. He was Killed in Action alongside many of them on 1st July, attacking South Sausage Trench just below the Willow Patch on Fricourt spur. In a nearby grave lies Captain Haswell whose toast saved the day. (See also Chapter 2, 'Final Preparations'.)

Bray-sur-Somme

In considering the rear areas south of Fricourt and Mametz it is impossible to avoid mentioning this village on the northern bank of the River Somme. Bray lies five miles south-east of Albert and due south of Fricourt, on the northern bank of one the enormous meandering loops which characterise the river's sedate progress. The most direct route to Bray from Albert is therefore south east along the D329.

Bray's history during the Great War is one of extensive involvement in the treatment, evacuation and burial of casualties. Consequently there are a number of cemeteries here including Bray British Military Cemetery to the north, Bray German Military Cemetery west of the town, as well as a French National Cemetery, which contains the grave of one British soldier, and a Communal Cemetery which contains the graves of three further British soldiers. The town is closely associated with the evacuation of casualties from XIII Corps' sphere of operations, east of Mametz, during the earliest days of the Battle of the

Major Stewart Loudoun-Shand helping his men across the parapet under fire. This illustration is taken from *Deeds that Thrill the Empire*.

Somme. During September's fighting the ground adjacent to the British Military Cemetery at Bray was used by the Main Dressing Station of XIV Corps. During 1917 the town was used by the 5th, 38th and 48th Casualty Clearing Stations. Bray was captured by the Germans in March 1918 and recaptured by an Australian battalion in August of that year. In the years after the war 203 of the 739 graves in Bray Military cemetery were concentrated there from battlefields both to the north and south of Bray.

Just outside the town are two smaller British Military cemeteries, both originally made during the 1918 fighting in this area. Bray Vale cemetery is on the east side of the D329 Albert road at the southern end of Happy Valley and contains 281 graves, of which 172 are unknown. A very considerable number of the known graves record men who served with the 47th (2nd London) Division and who were fighting towards Happy Valley on the morning of 22nd August during the Battle of Albert. On IGN maps the valley is noted as 'Vallee du Bois Ricourt'. The cemetery was expanded in 1923 by the concentration here of a number of 1916 graves removed from the Thiepval and Courcelette area. One of those graves removed from near to Thiepval belongs to Major George Gaffikin[2] who was killed during the

Bray German Military Cemetery.

36th Division's advance across Schwaben Redoubt north of Thiepval on 1st July 1916. Bray Hill cemetery lies on the west side of the D147 Bray to Fricourt road as you approach the plateau overlooking Happy Valley, which falls away to the west. Bray Hill cemetery contains the graves of 104 Allied soldiers, most of whom were killed during the period 22nd to the 26th August 1918.

Apart from being associated with the locations fought for by the soldiers of the 47th (2nd London) Division on 22nd August 1918 these cemeteries also contain the graves of a number of Australian soldiers serving with the 3rd Australian Division. The 3rd Australians were covering the right of the 47th Division's advance on 22nd August and were then involved in the fighting to capture Bray-sur-Somme on subsequent days. The cemetery on Bray Hill also contains the graves of a number of soldiers from the 58th Division. One particular place of interest adjacent to Bray Vale cemetery is the valley to the north, Happy Valley, which was the scene of an extraordinary and ill advised attack made by a squadron of the 1/1st Northumberland Hussars on 22nd August 1918 who rode up the valley in an attempt to capture the high ground on its eastern side towards the site of Bray Hill cemetery and Chataigneraie Farm to the north. Here, as they topped the eastern sides of the valley, the mounted soldiers were met by barbed wire entanglements, close range rifle and machine-gun fire as well as bombing from the air! The 23 surviving men were withdrawn to rally in the sunken lane west of the valley's entrance on the D329.

DERNANCOURT

Dernancourt village lies south-west of Albert in the Ancre valley. The communal cemetery in Dernancourt can be reached easily from Albert, along the D52 Corbie road. That road passes through the village of Dernancourt and then passes under the railway bridge. Ignore the road leading back immediately on your right, which is parallel to the railway, but take the next small road after a few further yards, leading away on the right of the road towards the entrance to the communal cemetery, through which the Military Extension can also be reached.

Dernancourt Communal Cemetery

The communal cemetery was used for burials between September 1915 and August 1916, and again during the retreat during March 1918. The graves belong to 124 UK soldiers and 3 Australians who were buried by Field Ambulances here. The entrance to the communal cemetery is located at the south-eastern end and the bulk of the military graves are to the right hand side of the cemetery. During August of 1916 the XV Corps' Main Dressing Station (MDS) was established here. The following month the 45th and 1/1st South Midlands Casualty Clearing Station (CCS) came here, followed by a succession of other CCSs. The duties of a CCS were, 'to retain all serious cases unfit to travel or requiring operation before being evacuated; to retain all slight cases likely to be fit for duty in a short period; to evacuate all others.'[3] The military extension, used after the August 1916 expansion of the medical facilities here, lies beyond the far end of the communal cemetery.

Dernancourt Communal Cemetery Extension (See page 165)

The finished appearance of this very large cemetery was created by the architect Edwin Lutyens. The two registers record 2,131 burials within the military extension. That extension had been started in August 1916 after the arrival of the XV Corps' Main Dressing Station here. That MDS operated by XV Corps was located along the right bank of the Ancre, on the expanse of open ground between the railway line and the river south-west of the village. Because of the location's long standing links with the RAMC's medical services, a significant number of the men buried here are described as having Died of

Wounds. Medical units, including a succession of CCSs, clustered in the vicinity until 26th March 1918 when Dernancourt was evacuated by the British forces. To bury the fatalities incurred at that time a small cemetery, known as Moor Cemetery, Edgehill, was used about half a mile to the west. After the war the graves of the 42 soldiers buried at Edgehill between the 23rd and the 25th March 1918, were concentrated into Dernancourt extension. During the period April to August 1918 a further cemetery was created at Buire-sur-l'Ancre, almost two miles to the west, and after the war the graves of the 65 soldiers buried there were also concentrated into Dernancourt extension. The village of Dernancourt was recaptured on 9th August that year, by the 12th Division and the 33rd American Division. In September the cemetery was again used for burials. Although the great majority of the men buried here came from the UK there are 418 Australian soldiers, 51 from New Zealand, 33 from South Africa, 8 from Canada, 1 from India and 1 from the British West Indies as well as a number of Indian and Chinese Labour Corps members and 3 German prisoners. One hundred and eighty graves are unknown and there are a number of special memorials to men believed or known to be buried here.

FRICOURT VILLAGE

Before the war Fricourt was a very substantial and relatively affluent village. The records show that it was inhabited by 593 people, of whom 185 were adult male electors. Apart from its many farmers, the village boasted a traditional array of professions amongst its inhabitants: surveyors, shop-keepers and inn-keepers, builders, laundry workers, game-keepers, bakers, manufacturers of 'Boutons de Nacre' (mother of pearl buttons), brewers, bricklayers, carpenters, wigmakers, tobacconists and the like. One legacy is that many ancient and discarded mussel shells are often found in the embankments, drilled with many holes which then became the mother of pearl buttons which were popular during that era!

Apart from the period up to 2nd July 1916 Fricourt village was again in German hands during the period 25th March until 26th August 1918. There are three military cemeteries close to Fricourt village. By far the largest is the German cemetery which is the product of a huge effort to concentrate some 17,000 graves from the Somme battlefield area. The German cemetery is a quite extraordinary testimony to the folly of war, maintaining a dignified and sombre presence on the north of the village, west of Fricourt wood. The two British cemeteries are much more intimate places, containing 132 graves at the British Cemetery on Bray Road and 210 at the New Military Cemetery. Rather misleadingly the register reports that Fricourt 'was attacked on the 1st July by the 17th Division...'. In fact these two places are closely linked with the attacks made upon Fricourt on 1st July 1916 by the 21st Division, attached to which were the men of 50 Brigade, detached from the 17th (Northern) Division, which included the 7th East Yorks and 10th West Yorks. There is a memorial bronze dedicated to the memory of the 17th Division within Fricourt's church. If the church doors are locked the key can usually be obtained from the cafe across the Rue du Raper. The road name derives from the village's recollection of the bravery of Major Raper who was killed within the village on 2nd July. In the immediate post war years the village and commune of Fricourt was 'adopted' by Ipswich and it was during the village's reconstruction that the Raper family paid for a series of stone tablets which now form part of the simple decor within the church. Until the 1960s Major Raper's grave lay outside the Bray Road cemetery on the opposite side of the road. After his family granted permission, his body was exhumed and re-buried within the Bray Road cemetery. However, the register still makes no mention of his grave other than to describe it as being found on the other side of the road.

Fricourt British Cemetery on the Bray Road also contains a poignant granite battle memorial erected after the war by members of the 7th Green Howards. The memorial records the names of the battalion's members killed during the period 1st-14th July.

One fascinating set of statistics, relating to the pre war communal cemetery next to the road junction south-west of Fricourt village, was derived from the census of traffic undertaken there by 'Traffic Control at Fricourt cemetery between 9.15 am, 21st July and 9.00 am, 22nd July'. [4] The cemetery referred to is on the D938 - D147 cross roads just south-west of Fricourt. At this junction two important routes, one from Contalmaison, the other from the Montauban and Mametz areas joined, some traffic being sent south towards Bray whilst other units drove

The granite memorial, erected after the war by members of the 7th Green Howards, found within the British Cemetery on the Bray Road.

Emile Belle's house in Fricourt, soon after the war and before reparations had begun to provide finance for the village's reconstruction.

west towards Albert. The census recorded the following data:

Troops	26,536
Guns	63
Gun Carriages	13
Motor cars	568
Buses and light tenders	95
Motor Cycles	617
Lorries	813
6 horse wagons	1,458
4 horse wagons	568

The list went on to include more than 5,000 horses being ridden individually, 330 motorised ambulances, more than 1,000 cyclists and a variety of other road users all competing for these busy stretches of road. The Official History notes that, 'from 10.00 pm to 4.00 am goggles had to be worn on account of 'tear gas' and this, combined with darkness, prevented the complete counting of infantry transport and ammunition columns.'!

Fricourt New Military Cemetery

Access is straight-forward. Take the lane leading west from the D147 as you leave the north of Fricourt. Keep to the left at the fork and later follow the path on your left down to the cemetery. This cemetery is much frequented by individual visitors and by larger parties, none of whom can fail to be moved by the special and intimate link which this place maintains with the past. The cemetery lies to the west of the northern end of Fricourt village and is in No Man's Land, adjacent to the German front line Konig Trench, just north of the British Tambour position. Fricourt New Military Cemetery is therefore constructed on the ground across which the 10th West Yorkshires attacked on the morning of 1st July, and over which C and D Companies of the 7th East Yorks also attacked at 2.33 pm that day, as part of the Subsidiary Attack on Fricourt.

The cemetery was created as a consequence of battlefield clearance undertaken by the survivors of the 10th West Yorks' attack and was created by four mass graves which were dug to expedite the work. There are also a few single graves dating from September 1916 but the majority date from 1st July. Fricourt New Military Cemetery contains 210 graves of which 159 belong to men who had attacked with the 10th West Yorkshires and 38 of men who belonged to the 7th East Yorks. Apart from the many ranks of ordinary soldiers who are commemorated here the cemetery also contains the grave of Lieutenant Colonel Arthur Dickson, buried next to his adjutant, who commanded the 10th West Yorkshires on 1st July.

Another grave, which maintains the literary associations which seem ever present in this area, is that of Lieutenant Victor Ratcliffe, 10th West Yorkshires. Ratcliffe had published a small book of poems in 1913 and, during the war, a periodical known as the *Microcosm* printed many of his poems, including some posthumously. Before the war he had studied in Heidelberg, describing the Germans as 'Everyman for himself and all for the state, that is the maxim here.' A few verses from one of his poems entitled 'At Sundown' serves to reveal the style of Ratcliffe's work and the inner tranquility which contrasts so starkly with the manner of his death.

The day put by his valiant shield
And cast him down.
His broken sword lay o'er a field
Of barley brown
And his bright sceptre and his crown
Were sunken in the river's heart.

His native tent of blue and gold
Was gathered in
I saw his torn flags o'er the wold:
And on the whin
High silence lit, and her next kin
Fair twilight spread her firefly wings.

The birds like secret thoughts lay still
Beneath the hush

**The grave of Lieutenant Vict
Ratcliffe, 10th West Yorkshire**

That held the sky and the long hill
And every bush
And floated o'er the river's rush
And held the windlets in her hand.

The two Yorkshire battalions were both Service units raised in Yorkshire as part of the K2 series. The 10th West Yorkshires were formed at York on 3rd September 1914 and were an eclectic mixture from York itself and other towns in the county such as Barnsley, Harrogate, Leeds and Sheffield as well as more distant origins in Sunderland, Durham and London. The 7th East Yorkshires had a similar spread of origins including many Yorkshire towns such as Middlesborough, Leeds, Halifax and Sheffield. They were formed at Beverley on 16th September 1914.

One grave now missing from the cemetery is that of Major James Leadbitter Knott, DSO. Major Knott was killed with his battalion on 1st July. After the war his body was exhumed from Fricourt New Military and taken to Ypres Reservoir cemetery where it was re-buried next to the body of his brother, Captain Henry Basil Knott. The two brothers were the sons of Sir James and Lady Knott of Close House, Wylam on Tyne. Their headstones in Ypres carry the inscription 'Devoted in life. In death not divided.' This small story reveals one of the reasons behind the decision to leave the British war dead in France. It had been the Knott family's intent to bring their sons' bodies home and they had pressed for some time with that aim in mind. In order to avoid the possibility of wealthy families offering money to ensure that bodies were returned to Britain or other Empire countries, the decision was made to leave all ranks of the war dead in situ, thus avoiding any possibility of conflict or rancour. The removal of James' body to Ypres was therefore something of a compromise.

Fricourt British Cemetery (Bray Road)

This particularly poignant but attractive cemetery is located just to the south of the village. The ground is marginally below the level of the road and lies on No Man's Land in the shallow vale of the Willow Stream. The northern boundary of the cemetery abuts to the German front line known as Fricourt Trench, which lay between Wing Corner to the south-east and Wicket Corner to the north-west. The cemetery was created by surviving members of the 7th Green Howards (Yorkshire Regiment) between the 5th and the 11th July 1916. There are some further burials from the period up to end of October that year

Fricourt British Cemetery, Bray Road, during the period immediately after the war.

as well as four graves from the 1918 fighting here. One hundred and thirty two soldiers are buried here, including one soldier commemorated on a special memorial. The 7th Green Howards buried 89 of their number here, 59 of those being in the two large graves in the middle of Row A.

From the cemetery there are fine all round views. Its sheltered location therefore makes the cemetery an informative and pleasant place to stay on a fine summer's day, taking the time to orientate yourself within the landscape. To the south-east, at the top of the visible slope, is the Bois Francais which Siegfried Sassoon knew so well. Running north is the location of the German and British front lines which crossed the Fricourt Spur before turning north-west to pass in front of La Boisselle. Here, at the Bray Road cemetery, you are just yards from the location of the traffic census referred to above. It is not difficult to visualise the sounds, dust and sights which must have accompanied such a massive movement of men and material, undertaken day and night throughout the Somme campaign, past Fricourt village.

Fricourt British Cemetery, Bray Road.

Fricourt German Cemetery

This is reached by walking north of the village along the D147 Contalmaison road. East of the cemetery lie Fricourt Wood and Fricourt Farm. There are excellent views to the south-west across towards the Tambour positions and the British New Military cemetery.

Fricourt German Military cemetery is the largest of all the burial grounds on this part of the 1916 Somme battlefield. There are approximately 5,000 named men commemorated here and each of the metal markers carries the names of at least two German soldiers. Because of the recriminatory atmosphere prevalent in the early 1920s Germany was allowed no opportunity to create a systematic group of cemeteries. Indeed, many German soldiers' bodies were destroyed by indiscriminate and unrecorded immolation, most of which was carried out at the quarries near Miraumont. The German cemetery here in Fricourt therefore represents the concentration of any remaining bodies from a huge area of the Somme battlefield and in total the cemetery now contains the remains of more than 17,000 men. One frequently rehearsed story has it that during the years of occupation after France was invaded in 1940 the Jewish graves within this cemetery, and many other German cemeteries, were desecrated. The consequence of this interpretation is that those graves have since been restored with a stone marker, each carrying the Star of David to properly record the part played by the Jewish community in Germany's war effort during the period 1914 - 18. By contrast some historians are adamant that Hitler, because of his small part within the story of the Great War, was in fact strongly set against any such actions which in any way diminished the 1914 - 1918 war's battlefield memorials.

However, one fact remains clear. The German cemeteries are dark and depressing places. The lack of a coherent method of financing and maintaining the cemeteries which house their war dead, allied to the fact of the German Army's ultimate failure, means that the vanquished German soldier has an inconspicuous grave by contrast with the bright and tranquil atmosphere of repose which surrounds the Commonwealth War Grave Commission's memorable cemeteries.

The Point 110 Cemeteries

The registers describing these two cemeteries are contained within the combined documents covering the Morlancourt Group of cemeteries. The two cemeteries at Point 110, so denoted because of the height above sea level of the British positions facing Bois Francais marked on contemporary trench maps, are reached easily from the road south of Fricourt. Cross the D938 and follow the CWGC signs pointing uphill. There are often signs denoting a 'Ball trap' here - an uncomfortable sounding Frenchism which points out that clay pigeon shooting is often undertaken here. As you approach Bois Francais, marked Bois d'Engremont on your IGN map, you are crossing the ground over which A and B Companies of the 20th Manchesters attacked on 1st July 1916. Passing the woods on your left you will soon come to a cross-roads. I suggest that if you are travelling by car you do not take it beyond this point since the track's surface in the vicinity of the cemeteries can be extremely rough. In the field by the wood are the remains of many craters. Don't be confused by the very symmetrical round structures which were dug just prior to the Second World War to house anti aircraft units whose purpose was to protect the aeroplane factory at Meaulte. If you care to glance within the grassy structures you will see the concrete bases upon which the guns turned. Walk straight ahead from where the first Point 110 cemetery can be seen some three hundred yards distant. By September of 1916 the high ground here was referred to as 'King George's Hill' after the monarch visited the area during his August tour of this part of the Somme battlefield.

Point 110 Old Military Cemetery *(the most northerly of the two cemeteries).*
This is also the site of Maple Redoubt. Point 110 Old Military Cemetery was begun by the French Army in February of 1915 and continued by British units from August 1915 to September 1916. The cemetery contains 100 graves of which three commemorate unknown soldiers. Noticeable here are the graves of a number of officers and men of the 174th Tunnelling Company, killed on 8th October 1915, and a C.S.M and a R.S.M of the 24th Manchesters, killed on 6th February 1916 amidst a period of heavy casualties suffered by that battalion on 6th and 7th of February. Bernard Adams, 1st RWF, looked across this tranquil scene one June morning in 1916 after spending the night in the front lines. The darkness had been brief and now was being superseded by a scene he described as 'one of the most perfect peace.' As the last

Looking back towards The Bois Francais (on the left) and Bois Allemand from the track leading past the Point 110 cemeteries to The Citadel.

vestiges of darkness slipped away Adams wished for some release from the stifling confines of the trenches.

'I went back and walked a little way along Park Lane until I came to a gap in the newly erected sand-bag parados. I went through a gap and into a little graveyard that had not been used now for several months. And there I stood in the open, completely hidden from the enemy, on the reverse slope of the hill. Below me were the dug-outs of 71 North, and away to the left those of the Citadel. Already I could see smoke curling up from the cookers. There was a faint mist still hanging about over the road there, that the strong light would soon dispel. On the hill-side opposite lay the familiar tracery of Redoubt A, and the white zigzag mark of Maidstone Avenue climbing up well to the left of it, until it disappeared over the ridge.'

If you have the relevant trench map to hand it is a simple matter to recreate in your mind's eye the view which began to unfold as the sun rose on Adams that morning.

'Close to my feet the meadow was full of buttercups and blue veronica, with occasional daisies starring the grass. And below, above, everywhere, it seemed, was the tremulous song of countless larks, rising, growing, swelling, till the air seemed full to breaking point.

And there was not a sound of war. Who could desecrate such a perfect June morning? I felt a mad impulse to run up and across into No Man's Land and cry out that such a day was made for lovers; that we were all enmeshed in a mad nightmare, that needed but a bold man's laugh to free us from its clutches!'

Yet the opening volleys of the Battle of the Somme were mere days away.

Point 110 New Military Cemetery

The New cemetery was begun by the French in May to July 1915 and continued in use by the British between February and July 1916. Twenty seven of the graves here belong to men who served with the 20th, 21st and 24th Manchesters, the last named being the 7th Division's pioneer battalion. The cemetery now contains 64 graves in all, but the most distinctive part is the line of soldiers belonging to the 24th Battalion of the Manchester Regiment, the Oldham Comrades, killed on 7th February 1916. This cemetery is also the burial place of David Thomas, a friend of both Siegfried Sassoon, Robert Graves and Adams. Both Sassoon and Graves were present when Thomas was

The view across Point 110 Old Military Cemetery, south of Bois Francais.

buried. Thomas's death moved Graves to write a poem entitled *Goliath and David*. Also buried nearby are 2nd Lieutenant David Pritchard (KiA 19/3/1916) and Captain Mervyn Richardson (DoW 19/3/1916), both of the 1st Royal Welsh Fusiliers and both known to and written about by the battalion's well known chroniclers.

The Citadel New Military Cemetery, Fricourt - Bray road

This can be reached on foot by heading southwards along the track leading from the two Point 110 cemeteries. Alternatively take the D147, signposted for Bray-sur-Somme, at the main cross roads with the D938 south of Fricourt. Follow this road for two kilometres, past the steep embankments on your left which sheltered Points 71 North and 71 South, before reaching the CWGC sign on your left. The track rises gently into a hollow which was the site of the Citadel camp. The first British burials here were made in August 1915, although the French used this location beforehand. Most of the graves date from before the Somme offensive, carried out by Field Ambulances working here. This cemetery is the site of Corporal Mick O'Brien's grave. Siegfried Sassoon, who had attempted to save O'Brien in those terrifying moments during the early hours of 24th May, described him as, 'a very fine man and had been with the battalion since November 1914. He was at Neuve Chapelle, Festubert and Loos.'

The New Military Cemetery at the Citadel is also the last resting place of a number of soldiers with high rank or who came from aristocratic backgrounds. Part of the explanation lies in the close links which the Guards Brigades had with this area during the September battles. Amongst those buried here is Guy Baring who, before the war, was a Conservative Member of Parliament. Serving as a Lieutenant Colonel, with the 1st Coldstream Guards, Baring was killed in action on 15th September. Another senior figure was Brigadier General Louis Phillpotts, CMG, DSO, killed in action on 8th September. One other grave which particularly stands out is that of Captain Alfred

Cuninghame, 2nd Grenadier Guards, who was the last survivor of the original battalion, serving in France continuously from 14th August 1914.

The Citadel Cemetery is reached through a distinctive and unusual entrance and contains 378 UK graves, only 15 being unknown because the vast majority of burials were carried out by Field Ambulances working here before the Battle of the Somme. Very many graves also belong to men who served with units of the 7th Division who were in and out of the lines south and east of Fricourt during the first half of 1916. If you have walked here in summer, along the dusty track running south from the Bois Francais, you will find that the trees which have matured within this cemetery provide welcome shelter from the heat of the sun.

MAMETZ VILLAGE

The village is the location of three cemeteries. Also to be found here is one recently erected (1995) memorial recording the exploits of the Manchester Pals battalions which served as part of the 7th Division. During the inter-war years a stone memorial to the 7th Division had been erected in Mametz but this was dismantled after damage incurred during the 1939 - 45 war.

Dantzig Alleg Cemetery[5]

Dantzig Alley is both one of the finest viewpoints and most interesting cemeteries on the Somme battlefield. It lies a short distance to the east of Mametz on the north side of the D64 Montauban road. Dantzig Alley cemetery receives relatively few visitors considering its size, importance and location but you will find that the panoramic views available here are well worth a detour. As already mentioned, a number of smaller cemeteries from the Fricourt and Mametz areas were concentrated here after the war, along with graves from Bottom Wood cemetery, Mametz German cemetery, Montauban Road Cemetery and Vernon Street Cemetery (the last two coming from the Carnoy area) together with a number of smaller outlying burial grounds. There are a minimal number of graves from the autumn of 1918, but the vast majority date from 1916. The cemetery contains more than 2,500 graves, of which 518 are unknown, and also contains a number of special memorials to men whose graves in other cemeteries were subsequently destroyed or lost because of shell fire. One of the soldiers buried here is Lieutenant Colonel Hugo Beaumont who commanded the 11th Queen's.

The cemetery's position is close to the site of two important German trenches which were attacked by the 22nd Manchesters and the 2nd Queen's of 91 Brigade on 1st July 1916. Opposite the cemetery, on the south side of the D64, was Danzig Alley Trench beyond which was Bucket Trench which the Manchesters took by 7.55 am. Running from the cemetery to the north-west was Fritz Trench across which a number of German counter attacks were launched in the morning. North of Dantzig Alley cemetery is Queen's Nullah where Major General Edward Charles Ingouville-Williams became the best known and most senior of the army's Somme casualties when he was killed at 7.00 pm on 22nd July. The 34th Division's Diary records the location as being at X.30.a.3,7 on the top of the bank of Queen's Nullah which is visible from the Dantzig Alley cemetery roughly half way to the southern tip of Mametz Wood. The northern views from Dantzig Alley therefore encompass a considerable panorama of the 1916 Somme battlefield past Contalmaison towards Pozieres. A short way to the east is the site of Pommiers Redoubt, captured by the 18th Division on the morning of 1st July. Dantzig Alley cemetery also marks the boundary between both the 7th and 18th Divisions and therefore that between XV and XIII Corps on 1st July 1916. Looking due west, across the valley of the Willow Stream, you can see Fricourt Wood past which lies the town of Albert.

Because of the post war concentrations from surrounding sites, Dantzig Alley contains many 1st July graves, mostly belonging to men and officers who served within the 7th Division but also the 18th and 30th Divisions. The cemetery was initially begun as a result of

The original memorial in Mametz, probably that of the 7th Division, 1920.

battlefield clearance work in early July, then continued by Field Ambulances and fighting units until November of 1916. It is also the site of a memorial seat and plaque dedicated to the memory of the Royal Welsh Fusilier units who fought in this vicinity and the many men who were killed in the fighting for Mametz Wood.

Dantzig Alley cemetery provides a fine vantage point from which to gain an understanding of the fighting which took place during the period 4th - 10th of July for the approaches to Mametz Wood. Although the final days of that fighting are outside the scope of this guide, Dantzig Alley cemetery provides such a fine vantage point that it is worth providing a few pointers to aid interpretation of the view from here. The attacks undertaken by 52 Brigade west of Mametz Wood, which I have already mentioned in Chapter 3, were organised in tandem with attacks made by the soldiers of 115 Brigade, part of the 38th (Welsh) Division who attacked the south-eastern aspect of Mametz Wood at 8.30 am this day, 7th July. The atmosphere surrounding those and subsequent events involving his battalion are vividly described by LLewelyn Wynn Griffith in his book, *Up to Mametz* published in 1931. Griffith was serving with the 15th Royal Welsh Fusiliers and initially observed many of the events from a vantage point at Pommiers Redoubt, just east of Dantzig Alley cemetery.

On the afternoon of 8th July the 38th Division were again ordered to attack the southern salient of Mametz Wood. In the following hours it was reported on several occasions that the Germans had withdrawn but any patrols which went out into the open north of Queen's Nullah drew heavy fire from machine guns sited in the wood's perimeters. In the darkness of the following early morning, 9th July, it proved impossible to get even small groups of men forward over ground within the Willow Stream valley and Queen's Nullah areas which were pitted with shell holes and littered with loose barbed wire.[6] Later that

The grave of Captain Alfred Bland, Killed in Action on 1st July whilst serving with the 22nd Manchesters. He had been one of the finest correspondents of the war in a series of vivid letters written to his wife. (See Chapter 2 and the section dealing with the 22nd Manchesters' raid on Bulgar Point.)

morning the 38th Division's commanding officer was replaced by Major General H.E.Watts from the 7th Division on the grounds that he knew the terrain. Later that day Watts ordered a further attack, to be undertaken by the 38th Division's men on the south and south-eastern aspects of Mametz Wood and by the 17th Division's men against Wood Support trench on the south-west of the wood.[7] As a result of those events the fighting then moved within the terrible confines of Mametz Wood and well beyond the scope of this guide.

The Devonshire Cemetery

On 1st July 1916 the Devons were part of 20 Brigade's attack. That Brigade was due to move in a north-westerly direction past the southern end of Mametz village. The Devonshire cemetery and the fields to its south and west are a fine vantage point from which to appreciate those events. The cemetery has become a much frequented stopping place for individuals and parties visiting the Somme. The reason is clear in that the cemetery possesses an intimate privacy allied to a panoramic view, both of which are given emotive substance from the personal and anecdotal stories associated with this part of the front line.

Access from the D938 Albert - Peronne road is simple. On your right as you leave the road is a chalk quarry, the use of which is in danger of undermining the Devonshire cemetery. Entry is gained along a well trodden and rather worn pathway which leads up an embankment. Once there you are looking along the site of the 9th Devon's front line trench, from above which Captain Duncan Martin led A Company into their attack that fateful morning. On the right of the 9th Devons were the 2nd Gordon Highlanders and their cemetery can be seen on the north-eastern side of the D938. To the left of the Devons were the 2nd Borders who formed the left hand unit of the 7th Division. The Border's task was to form a defensive flank facing Fricourt prior to the Subsidiary Attack which was to be ordered later that day.

Following the attack by the 9th Devons, and that of the 8th Battalion in support, the survivors buried the regiment's dead here in the front line trench. That service took place on 4th July. Ten of the Devon's men were unidentifiable. The cemetery contains one officer of the 8th Battalion who had been killed on 28th June, along with three officers and 34 other ranks who were killed on 1st July. The 9th Battalion's casualties on 1st July included six officers and 116 other ranks who are buried here, together with one officer of the 11th Battalion, 2nd

The view towards Mametz Wood from the vantage point of the memorial seat at the rear of Dantzig Alley cemetery.

Lieutenant William Riddle, who was also killed here that day. The cemetery also contains the graves of two men killed later in the Somme battles, whilst serving with B Battery, 92 Brigade RFA.

One officer buried here has a distinctive literary association. He was Lieutenant William Noel Hodgson of the 9th Battalion. William Hodgson was the son of the Right Reverend Henry Hodgson who was the Bishop of Saint Edmundsbury and Ipswich. Lieutenant Hodgson had already been mentioned in despatches before being awarded the Military Cross in October 1915. In the first decade of the twentieth century William Hodgson had been educated at Durham School, completing his education at Christ Church College, Oxford. Hodgson's best known and finest poem, written just hours before his death, was entitled 'Before Action'. For many days the 23 year old Lieutenant William Hodgson had observed the massive British artillery barrage falling on Mametz, contemplating the moments when the barrage's end would signify the start of the battle. On 29th June, crouched in a filthy dug-out somewhere in the trenches which snaked around Mansell Copse, Hodgson wrote with an unerring poignancy about the forthcoming days and the vivid, terrible contrast with those things that he held dear.

> I, that on my familiar hill
>   Saw with uncomprehending eyes
> A hundred of thy sunsets spill
>   Their fresh and sanguine sacrifice,
> Ere the sun swings his noonday sword
>   Must say good-bye to all of this;-
> By all delights that I shall miss,
>   Help me to die, O Lord

The poem, of which this is the last verse, encapsulates a sense of

131

premonition and inevitability. Most poignantly, in the line 'By all delights that I shall miss', William Hodgson's words gave form to the idea that many men would die without the experience and satisfaction of all that youth should have brought to them. After Hodgson's death a posthumous volume of his work was published under the title *Verse and Prose in Peace and War*.

Another grave within the Devonshire cemetery also reveals the terrible presentiment of death which many soldiers had to overcome before action. As already mentioned Captain Martin was due to lead A Company's attack on the right of the 9th Devon's frontage. Before the event he had taken home leave. During those days he had employed his professional artist's eye for form and structure to create a detailed reconstruction of the area's topography in plasticine. Martin saw that the shallow bowl or valley north of their trench in Mansell Copse was under direct observation from the Shrine and Shrine Alley and that the machine-guns located there would pour a terrible and direct enfilade into the right of his company as they filed out from the protection of Mansell Copse. His prediction was entirely accurate. Martin and his men were seen even before leaving the shelter of Mansell Copse's shattered trees and many were cut down even before they spilled out into the valley below. Captain Martin is buried in grave A1 near to many of his own company's men. The other company making the initial assault fared far better, being above the most confined part of the valley and further from the Shrine Alley positions, being able to cross Danube Trench and its supports as they moved forward towards the western end of Mametz village.

The Gordon Cemetery (See page 165)

This cemetery lies on the left of the D938 just past the Devonshire cemetery as you travel in the direction of Peronne. Its distinctive construction lends an air of considerable beauty and tranquility to its purpose. In the years immediately after the Great War the Albert - Peronne light railway was reconstructed and ran between the road and the cemetery boundary.

The 2nd Gordon Highlanders were set the task of attacking across the southern approaches of Mametz over Shrine Alley in the direction of Danzig Alley to the west of the village. This attack was therefore undertaken parallel to the road and the Albert–Peronne light railway line. Unlike the Devons the Gordons' dead were buried in the British support trench called Queen's Road, between the site of two communication trenches known as 66 Street and 67 Street. The cemetery contains the graves of six officers and 93 other ranks of their battalion, together with three artillerymen who were killed on the 8th July. The bulk of the headstones have been arranged in two semi-circles around the base of the Great Cross.

MEAULTE VILLAGE

If you are travelling from Albert take the D42 Meaulte - Morlancourt road and turn left onto the main street which runs the length of Meaulte village. Shortly afterwards turn right, following the CWGC sign, along the minor road leading in the direction of Etinehem where you will find the Military Cemetery, 500 yards south of Meaulte, on the right hand side of the road.

The cemetery contains almost three hundred graves, twenty one of which are unknown. There is a special memorial within the cemetery to eleven UK soldiers believed to be buried within the cemetery confines. After the war two significant nearby cemeteries were concentrated into Meaulte Military Cemetery. The first was Sandpit Cemetery, which was located east of Meaulte at E.18.d.3,3. Also brought here were the graves from Meaulte Triangle Cemetery which was in E22, between the village and the light railway crossing on the Morlancourt road.

The village of Meaulte was occupied by British troops, who lived rather uneasily alongside three quarters of its pre-war population, between 1915 and 26th March 1918. On that date the village was evacuated after a rearguard fight involving the 9th (Scottish) Division. Meaulte was re-captured on 22nd August 1918, by soldiers serving with the 12th (Eastern) Division. As a consequence, apart from the 1915-16 graves, there are many graves dating from the third week in August 1918. Meaulte Military Cemetery therefore reveals a very accurate chronology of the British part in the fighting on the Somme during the Great War.

One grave of note that you might find of special interest is that of Lieutenant Richard William Jennings, 10th Worcesters. Although he died of wounds received at La Boiselle on 3rd July, it was not before he had dictated an account of the extraordinary bravery of Private Thomas Turrall who was awarded the Victoria Cross following his brave attempts to save Lieutenant Jennings' life.[8] Jennings himself was a fine soldier and officer. Before the war he had qualified as a solicitor having attended Cambridge University where he was Lightweight Boxing Champion during 1909-10.

Grove Town Cemetery

Getting to Grove Town from Meaulte Military Cemetery is straightforward. Continue along the minor road towards Etinehem in a south easterly direction. At the first cross-roads after one kilometre go straight ahead but at the next junction, after a further kilometre, turn left and the lane will bring you to Grove Town Cemetery. The cemetery can also be accessed from the D329 Albert - Bray road. Take the lane opposite the aerodrome for one kilometre and thence the rough track on your left.

A short glance at the many rows of headstones within Grove Town cemetery will tell you that the history of this burial ground is not the same as its neighbour, Meaulte Military Cemetery further north-westwards in the direction of Meaulte village. Grove Town was established by the 34th and 2/2nd London Casualty Clearing Station in September 1916. The two CCSs were moved in April 1917 and only a small number of further burials were made here, during August and September 1918. This was an important location for the evacuation of the wounded from the First Battle of the Somme, being close to the site of the Dernancourt–Loop railway line used by ambulance trains throughout this period. As a consequence of these circumstances many graves belong to men recorded as having Died of Wounds. The graves are therefore grouped in a regular manner rather than the more haphazard patterns which characterise some battlefield cemeteries. This is a large cemetery containing almost 1,400 Allied graves together with those of 34 German prisoners. One of the men buried here was Sergeant Leslie Coulson, who was part of the area's literary associations, being the author of a book published posthumously, *From an Outpost and Other Poems*.

MORLANCOURT

This village can be reached on either the D42 road which runs south-west from Albert past the western end of Meaulte or via the D52 running through Dernancourt. Throughout the first three and a half years of war Morlancourt was a quiet location, much appreciated by the troops who used its restful and plentiful supply of clean billets. The lie of the land meant that the village was sheltered from observation and was, in any case, beyond the range of German guns. Throughout much of 1916 the place was the scene of operations for Field Ambulances. Morlancourt was captured by the German army in late March 1918 and recaptured by the British following the advances made during the Battle of Amiens during August that year, after which operations focused on the battle to retake Meaulte and Albert. Ville-sur-Ancre is included in the Morlancourt group of cemeteries.

Morlancourt British Cemetery Number 1

This cemetery was made on the west side of the village by Field Ambulances, operating on the low ground in front of the cemetery during June and July 1916. The plot is a slender finger of ground which looks across fields towards the western aspect of Morlancourt village. My impression is that this distinctive cemetery is visited very infrequently. The register box has been filled with stone making a record of people's visits impossible to ascertain. However, this lonely location holds much interest in that it was the start of the Plateau railway line's ascent onto the higher ground east of Morlancourt towards Grove Town sidings. Many of the soldiers buried here at Morlancourt Number 1 are known to have Died of Wounds received during the height of the early Somme battles. There are 75 soldiers buried here, four of whom are unknown. They include Lieutenant Colonel Flower of the Royal Welsh Fusiliers and a number of men serving with the Manchester Pals in the Mametz and Montauban areas.

Morlancourt British Cemetery Number 2 (See page 165)

This cemetery lies next to the rough track leading back towards Ville-sur-Ancre. Unlike Morlancourt British Cemetery Number 1 the 56 graves in this cemetery were dug in August 1918 and the bulk of those graves belong to men who served within units of the 12th (Eastern) Division. Morlancourt village itself was re-captured on 9th August, the second day of the great offensive operation undertaken by Fourth Army known as the Battle of Amiens 1918. The cost of the subsequent advance on 22nd and 23rd August (the Battle of Albert) along the ridge to the east of Morlancourt towards Happy Valley and Bray is represented by a number of graves of men killed during those two days, at least 19 of whom were the 18 and 19 year olds upon whom the British divisions were by this time so dependant.[9] The cemetery is surrounded by a distinctive flint stone wall and access is gained across a small bridge which lends a very unusual and attractive aspect to the cemetery's appearance.

Ville-sur-Ancre communal and military extension

Within the Morlancourt group of cemeteries there is also much merit in looking at Ville-sur-Ancre communal cemetery and its military extension. The communal cemetery was enlarged by the addition of a number of British and Empire graves, the bulk of which date from the first half of 1916, amongst whom are ten men who served with the 97th Field Company, Royal Engineers, who were killed in action on 26th June 1916. During the German spring offensive of 1918 Ville-sur-Ancre marked the point at which the British army was able to re-establish a line south-west of the 1916 Somme battlefield and halt the German advance towards Amiens.

The military extension lies to the south of the communal cemetery. The bulk of the graves are of men killed during the period 7th - 12th August 1918, although there are some exceptions such as Private John South and Sergeant John Wilding, both of whom were Salford Pals, killed in action on 1st July 1916 at Thiepval. These last two mentioned are examples of men whose bodies lay undiscovered until post war battlefield clearance work brought their remains to light. However, the date 8th August is significant in that it marks the start of the Battle of Amiens 1918 when, at 4.20 am, the Fourth Army began its relentless quest for victory which is often characterised by the phrase 'The Last Hundred Days'. As is the case at Morlancourt British Cemetery Number 2 the Ville-sur-Ancre cemetery contains the graves of an extraordinarily high proportion of the 18 and 19 year old soldiers, the men of 18 of 1918.

1. There is an inconsistency between the Official History's spelling of Mansell Copse and the Imperial War Grave Commission's spelling of Mansel Copse. I have used the Mansell form throughout.
2. See Stedman, *Thiepval*, and also *Crozier, A Brasshat in No Man's Land*.
3. *Official History. Military Operations, France and Belgium, 1916. Vol 1*. pp 281.
4. *Official History. Military Operations, France and Belgium, 1916. Vol 1*. pp 283.
5. There is an inconsistency in the Official History's spelling of the name Danzig Alley, and that used by the Imperial War Graves Commission after the war in establishing Dantzig Alley cemetery. I have used the 'Danzig' form throughout the rest of the text but have used the 'Dantzig' form when describing the cemetery in this entry within Chapter 5.
6. The attacks made on these approaches to Mametz Wood during 8th July and subsequent days are dealt with in Griffiths' book between pages 207 and 228 but more properly form the subject matter of the guide which deals with Mametz Wood.
7. These events were marked by terrible casualties and great heroism and are fully dealt with in the *Official History, 1916 Volume II*, pages 49 onwards.
8. See Stedman, *La Boisselle*, 1997, Leo Cooper, Pen & Sword Books.
9. In reality many more than the 19 which I have mentioned may have been 18 or 19 years of age since their ages are not mentioned upon their headstones or within the cemetery register entries.

Chapter Six.

TWO TOURS AND FIVE WALKS WITHIN THE AREA

This section of the guide provides a series of tours and walks. The first of these is a general tour, too long to undertake except by cycle, car or coach, designed to make you familiar with the main geographic features and sites of historic interest to be found within the area. Primarily this guide is concerned with the area attacked by the troops comprising the three divisions of XV Corps on 1st July 1916, although much attention has also been paid to the rear areas, used for the assembly of men and materials, as well as to the impact which the fighting during 1918 had on these locations. Because the area covered by this guide is extensive those of you with cycles might consider bringing them along. The locations around Fricourt certainly lend themselves well to exploration on two wheels, especially during the summer months. As a general rule of thumb a walk described as taking roughly three hours should be capable of being completed on a mountain cycle in one quarter of that time, depending entirely, of course, on how long you care to dwell at the many places of interest. The detailed walks described here will allow you to develop an intimate understanding of particular locations, all of which are contained within what is perhaps the most attractively rural landscape within the British part of the Somme battlefield. Whilst stopping at places of interest I suggest that you periodically cross reference with the relevant sections of historical narrative and cemetery entries. I have also included a car or cycle tour of some of the rear areas to the south-west of the 1916 battlefield, places which were themselves the scene of severe fighting both during the spring and late summer of 1918.

The town of Albert

Albert is closely linked with its agricultural hinterland. It is a market town and maintains a main line railway station on the line running from Paris and Amiens to Arras and Lille. Before the Great War a series of narrow gauge railway lines linked Albert to its nearby satellite villages whose produce was distributed via the main line rail network towards Paris and Lille. An example was the Albert - Peronne narrow gauge line which ran south of Fricourt and Mametz and thence along the valley between the Devonshire and Gordon cemeteries near Mansell Copse. Albert had also built a reputation for the manufacture of Singer sewing machines and as the home of machine tool manufacturing in France and was therefore a potentially valuable asset to the invading German Army. To this day that specialised engineering link is maintained by the town's motto, *'Vis Mea Ferrum'* - 'My strength is in Iron', and by the Aerospatiale aircraft factory at Meaulte, just south of Albert.

During the period 1914 - 1916 Albert's station and shunting yards were within range of the German artillery and the main British railhead was therefore located at Dernancourt which is also covered by this guide. Albert was held by French forces throughout the period from September 1914 until it passed into British control in the summer of 1915. The town was captured by the Germans, during their spring offensive, on 26th March 1918. However, Albert was subsequently re-captured on the 22nd August that year, during the second Battle of Albert, and many casualties buried in the cemeteries covered by this guide bear witness to the severity of that battle. Although some buildings on the west of Albert had remained relatively unscathed during the earlier periods of war, the bombardment by the British artillery prior to Albert's recapture had resulted in the total devastation of the few remaining structures. After the war the town, like so many on the Somme, was adopted by a British city, in this case Birmingham whose legacy lies along the Rue Birmingham adjacent to the Basilica.

The town of Albert also plays host to an excellent museum, the *Musee des Abris* (Rue a Godin, telephone 00 33 322 75 16 17), which details the impact of the Great War on this area. The museum entrance is found next to the Byzantine styled basilica. The evocative reconstructions recreate battlefield scenes in the alcoves and tunnels which run under the area. Many of these tunnels were dug during 1938 in anticipation of German bombing of the aircraft factory at Meaulte. That preparation is mirrored in the anti-aircraft gun positions which were prepared along Siegfried Sassoon's old haunts south of Bois Francais. Older parts of the subterranean complex date back as far as the 16th century. The museum is open March to November between 10 and noon and 2 until 6 pm and is well worth a visit.

On the opposite side of the main square you will find the Tourist Office (Office de Tourisme, Syndicat d'Initiative, 9 Rue Gambetta, telephone 00 33 322 75 16 42) where English is spoken. Here you can obtain details of accommodation, directions, restaurants and all the facilities for recreation and tours which are to be found in this area.

A general tour of the area to familiarise yourself with the main features around the area covered by this guide.

This tour is suitable for cars and coaches. If you stop at all the suggested locations the circuit may well take four hours to complete. I suggest that you make use of the relevant IGN maps. The Green series 1:100,000 Laon - Arras sheet will suffice, but more detail can be gleaned by making use of the Blue series 1:25,000 sheets, the most useful being 2408 west to cover the Albert, Meaulte, Dernancourt and Morlancourt areas, which were behind the British lines before the First Battle of the Somme, and 2408 east to cover Fricourt, Mametz and Bray-sur-Somme. However, the map below will help if you have been unable to obtain the IGN sheets.

Map 16. Route map for the general tour of the area.

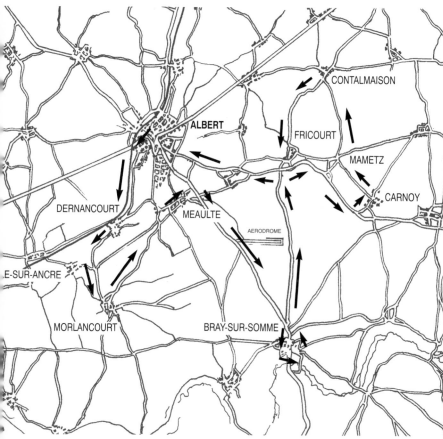

A suitable starting point is Albert. Take the D929 running south-west in the direction of Amiens. Before reaching the outskirts take the left fork onto the D52 in the direction of Dernancourt. From 1915 until the German spring offensive of 1918 this road was free from shellfire and the village of Dernancourt was therefore the centre for British railhead and medical activity in the area. However Albert contained very few civilians since the bulk of the town was within range of the German guns in Mametz Wood and whose shellfall could be seen by observers operating on the Pozieres ridge and the Fricourt spur.

The quartermastering and medical facilities occupied the wide expanse of sheltered ground either side of the railway line south-west of Dernancourt village. The medical facilities were mostly on the south side of the line whilst to the north there were clusters of sidings where the unloading of supplies could be undertaken. Pass down the main street of Dernancourt until the western end of the village where you can take a left turn towards the church. However, if you intend to visit the site of Dernancourt communal cemetery and the Military Extension this is the time to do so by avoiding the left turn and passing under the railway, where you bear round to the left and then take the lane on your right into the cemetery. If you do not intend to visit the cemetery then continue down to the church, turning right there and keeping to the narrow lane which crosses the River Ancre in the direction of Ville-sur-Ancre. One kilometre after crossing the bridge you will reach the D120. Turn left and then immediately right in the direction of Morlancourt.

Morlancourt village was well known to the 7th Division's soldiers

Morlancourt village today.

and often written about by the likes of Sassoon, Graves and Adams. The village is sheltered in a pleasing conjunction of three valleys. The undamaged billets here were described as clean and the place was enjoyed by soldiers seeking a respite from the rigours of the front lines. The village is the location of two very fine but seemingly infrequently visited British Military cemeteries, one dating from 1916, the other from 1918. This may be an ideal opportunity to visit these.

Continuing the general tour, from Morlancourt's communal cemetery take the road running north-east in the direction of Meaulte. This road, the D42, rises up across a spur of higher ground before dropping down towards the village of Meaulte, some 3 kilometres distant. Today Meaulte is the home of this area's long standing links with the aerospace industry, but in 1916 it had a reputation of providing some of the filthiest and most lice ridden of all billets on the western front. The village was then

This well known photograph shows Sir Douglas Haig in animated conversation with Lloyd George, whilst General Joffre looks on from between the two men. They are at XIV Corps Headquarters at Meaulte on 12th September, 1916.

still occupied by most of the pre-war inhabitants as well as thousands of soldiers. It was a volcanic mix and the men constantly complained of the profiteering and ill considered behaviour of the villagers. Happily today things are very different. During the early months of 1916 this village was within range of the German gunners but the British maintained extensive railway sidings south-west of the village on the line running from Dernancourt through to The Loop. Later in 1916, as the fighting moved eastwards, the railway facilities at Meaulte were greatly expanded with the construction of the Meaulte–Martinpuich line which ran north-eastwards through Becordel, Becourt, Fricourt, along the Willow Stream valley past Bottom Wood and up towards the villages of Bazentin and Longueval. By that time there were at least 35 sidings for the storage and movement of locomotives and wagons in the Meaulte–Vivier Mill area!

Meaulte gives access to two important cemeteries and this may be an opportunity to visit those places. The entry in this guide's cemeteries section gives details of access. Now pass through Meaulte village main street and at the far end turn right opposite the site of the aircraft factory onto the D329 Bray road. The football pitch south of the factory was the site of Sandpit encampment where a cemetery was constructed during the war. The graves from the Sandpit were later exhumed and re-buried at Meaulte Military cemetery. Continue along the D329 past the aerodrome's runway on your left. After about one and a half further kilometres you will cross the site of the old Plateau Line railway which then skirted the northern end of Happy Valley before crossing the Bray Fricourt road and entering the vicinity of The Loop. Carry on and before reaching Bray you will reach Bray Vale cemetery on your left. The valley which leads away to the north is Happy Valley which was a vast encampment and bivouac where reserve units of the Fourth Army were rested after battle and held in reserve before being sent forward. The valley is accessible from the track which leads away from the road next to the cemetery. During 1916 the slopes at the northern end of Happy Valley were lined with artillery units firing on the German held villages of Fricourt and Mametz along with positions in Mametz Wood and Fricourt Wood. A further kilometre will lead you into the small town of Bray-sur-Somme. If you intend to visit any of the cemeteries here this is a good opportunity since Bray marks the very southern limit of this guide and lies some distance from the focus of the action in and around Fricourt and Mametz.

Now head north from Bray along the D147 Fricourt road. For the first kilometre or so the road rises out of the Somme valley and a fine view reveals itself to the south across the river valley. Two kilometres from the town centre lies Bray Hill cemetery on the left of the road. One kilometre past Bray Hill you will come to Chataigneraie farm on your left. Just before the farm is a track on the right side of the D147. Due east of the entrance to that track, some 800 metres distant, is the horseshoe shaped embankment upon which the rail interchange known as The Loop stood. If you intend to visit this area now turn off the D147, just south of Chataigneraie Farm, where there is space to park your vehicle. Don't be fooled by the IGN maps which show a track running eastwards across the fields here - it doesn't exist! Nevertheless, immediately walk towards the east, following the course

The King, The Prince of Wales, and Generals Rawlinson and Congreve at King George's Hill, Fricourt, 10th August 1916. This sombre moment was captured by the photographer as the party stood thoughtfully at the grave of an unknown British soldier.

of the overhead cables which duplicate the course of the old track, and strike out for roughly 700 metres until you reach a junction with the Bray-Mametz lane. Facing you the cuttings and embankments of The Loop are still clearly visible to the south-east. One kilometre east is Bronfay Farm which lies within the confines of the Montauban - Carnoy–Maricourt area. Now continue with the general tour by driving northwards along the D147 from where you will soon see a shallow valley on your right containing a large British cemetery. This is the site of the Citadel camp. The road continues northwards and eventually comes to the D938 south of Fricourt.

On your left, as you approach the D938 junction, is the communal cemetery where the extraordinary traffic survey on 22nd July 1916 was undertaken. The German lines north of here past the Tambour positions were attacked by the 21st Division on the 1st July 1916. East of here was the 7th Division's sphere of operations. Turn right onto the D938 in the direction of Peronne. After two kilometres you will pass the site of the Devonshire cemetery on your right and the Gordon cemetery on your left. Due north of here lies Mametz village. Carry on past the cemeteries for a further kilometre then turn left towards Carnoy, which was behind the lines of the 18th Division. Caftet Wood (Bois Caffet on your IGN map), on the north side of this junction, is just beyond the eastern limits of this guide. Pass through the village of Carnoy and take the left turn, at the northern end of the village, in the direction of Mametz. After 500 metres you will come to a slight embankment either side of the road. This was known to the British troops as The Mound and formed the site of the 22nd Manchesters' front line from which they attacked on 1st July as the extreme right hand unit of the 7th Division. On the Manchesters' right, to the east, were 11th Royal Fusiliers of the 18th Division. Continue into Mametz village, crossing the D64 road at the site of the village war memorial and head north along the minor road leading towards Contalmaison. As you enter the valley of the Willow Stream take the left fork. The right fork leads to Queen's Nullah, on the right, where Major General Edward Charles Ingouville-Williams, commanding the 34th Division, was killed[1]. Continue towards Contalmaison past Bottom Wood on your left and the imposing sight of Mametz Wood on your right. Just outside Contalmaison is the communal cemetery which is just beyond the northernmost limit of this guide. Drop down towards Contalmaison along the sunken lane and turn left back towards Fricourt along the D147.

As the D147 begins to swing south you have come within the 21st Division's sphere of operations on 1st July. On the right of the road is Round Wood. Moving closer to Fricourt the road passes Lozenge Wood on your left where a lane leads to Fricourt Farm (Ferme du Bois). A few metres further will take you past the German Military cemetery, again on your left. Pass through Fricourt and past the Bray Road cemetery, on your right, which marks the German front line known as Fricourt Trench. Looking south east from here you can see up the rise towards Bois Francais on the skyline, south of which are the Point 110 cemeteries. Now turn right onto the D938 from where you can return to Albert.

WALK ONE
Bois Francais, Points 110, the Citadel and The Loop

This is a very rewarding but lengthy journey. I suggest that, if travelling on foot, you should set aside a full morning or afternoon of three hours to enjoy the sights and tranquillity which this area brings.

A suitable starting point is the foot of the lane leading up towards Bois Francais *(Bois d'Engremont)* from the southern limits of Fricourt village. This was Wing Corner and it was here that men of A Company of the 1st Royal Welsh Fusiliers attacked alongside the 20th Manchesters during the first moments of the Subsidiary Attack on Fricourt at 2.30 pm on 1st July. A few yards to the left of the sunken

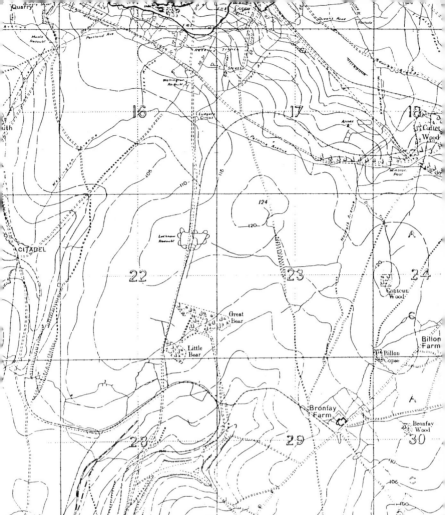

Map 17. The Bois Francais - Point 110 - Citadel - Loop areas from the 1:10,000 Trench map.

road, as you walk uphill, a small path follows the line of the German front line known as Sunken Trench. Towards the top of the slope you come within the shelter of the trees and within those trees much

Photograph. Looking past Point 110 Old Military Cemetery in the direction of its twin cemetery, Point 110 New, and site of The Citadel encampment.

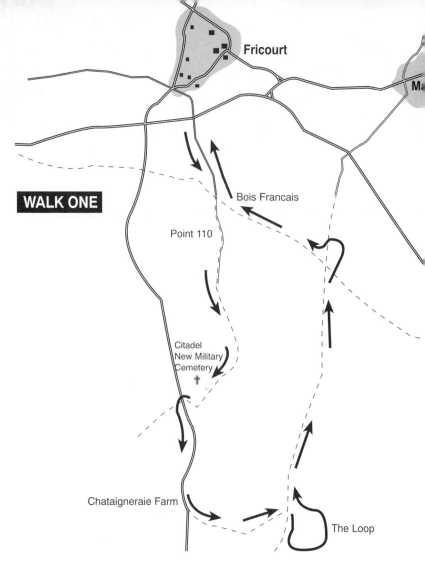

Map 18. Route Map for Walk One.

quarrying for chalk has been undertaken over many years. The lane rises onto open land past the trees and here the ground is cratered and distorted by the effects of the many mines which were detonated here during 1915 and the first six months of 1916.

Walking south you will come to a small cross-roads where you should carry on ahead towards the Point 110 cemeteries. This track was the site of Park Lane communication trench which ran down to Maple Redoubt which was used as a Battalion HQ by many units here, the 1st Royal Welsh's writers frequently mentioning the trenches and

The view towards Bray-sur-Somme from the vicinity of The Loop. The scars left by the railway sidings on both sides of the valley are still clearly visible today.

atmosphere in this vicinity. There were many shell-proof shelters to the south-west, denoted on trench maps as Point 71 North and Point 71 South. The shelters were dug into the road embankment of the Bray - Fricourt road and could be reached from Maple Redoubt by two communication trenches, Canterbury Avenue and Weymouth Avenue. In spring and autumn the chalk spoil on the surface makes Maple Redoubt easily visible as you approach on the track. Moving past Maple Redoubt on your left the first cemetery you come to is Point 110 Old Military, on the right. This is an appropriate moment to remind yourself of the material in the cemeteries section of this guide as well as the description which deals with this area, during the winter of 1915 and the spring of 1916, found at the start of Chapter 2. The track continues south past Point 110 New Military cemetery and thence begins to drop down in a south-westerly direction through the confines of the Citadel encampment. Within the valley here is the Citadel New Military cemetery after which the track reaches the D147 Bray - Fricourt road.

Turn left onto the D147 until you pass Chataigneraie Farm, just south of which turn left onto a track. The IGN maps show another track leading away to the east. Don't be fooled–this track has long since ceased to exist! However, its course is replicated by overhead telegraph cables which follow the course of the Plateau line to the site of The Loop. A narrow gauge railway line created and used by troops of the 7th Division in the spring of 1916 ran from The Loop southwards towards Bray. Later on during the battle that line was extended northwards in the direction of Fricourt and beyond. Carry along the course of the overhead wires and the Plateau line until you come to a 'T' junction facing the cuttings and embankments of The Loop. These are easily accessible and amongst them you can readily imagine the intense activity which characterised this location during the Battle of the Somme. To the south is a fine view towards Bray. In the early morning or late afternoon light the many sidings and embankments which cluttered the area are clearly visible. To the east lies Bronfay Farm which lay behind the 18th and 30th Division's sphere of operations on 1st July 1916.

Return to the 'T' junction and proceed due north across the plateau. One of the pre-war narrow gauge lines led, parallel to this track, northwards to Wellington Redoubt overlooking Mametz. Five hundred metres north of The Loop is a small woodland on your right, known to the troops as the Great Bear because of its distinctive shape. Just north of the Great Bear was an important position known as Lucknow Redoubt through which the pre-war railway line ran. It was here at Lucknow Redoubt that the 8th Devons, 2nd Royal Warwicks and 2nd Royal Irish were held ready to move up in support before the 7th Division's attacks on 1st July. One and a half kilometres of level walking north from The Loop will bring you to another cross-roads which was the site of Wellington Redoubt. Again the 7th Division's men were fully stretched in the weeks prior to the Big Push in the preparation of the rail line running from The Loop up to Wellington Redoubt.

It is worth noting that three hundred and fifty metres north of Wellington Redoubt lay the trenches from which the 2nd Borders attacked on 1st July. This area is very interesting and revealing. The Border battalion was the left hand unit of the main attack made by the 7th Division. The Borders task was to cross Danube Trench, which lay across the shallow valley west of Mansell Copse, and then wheel left across Shrine Alley, passing Hidden Wood before making a defensive flank facing Fricourt. You will notice that north-west of Wellington Redoubt the area of No Man's Land is extensively cratered and pocked by four mines which were detonated during the last moments before the attacks made by the Borders.

At 7.30 am there was no battalion attack to the left of the Borders across this cratered area. Return to the lane and stroll west past the site of the quarry back towards Bois Francais. Six hundred metres north-west of Wellington Redoubt you will come to the area attacked by C Company of the 20th Manchesters as part of the 2.30 pm Subsidiary Attack on Fricourt. Note that the anti-aircraft emplacements in this area are nothing to do with the Great War, rather they were dug in 1939 in anticipation of another invasion. At the cross-roads adjacent to Bois Francais turn right and thence down the slope back towards Fricourt. The German front line here followed a course just to the east of this lane down to the cross-roads. Take in the views here, north towards La

148

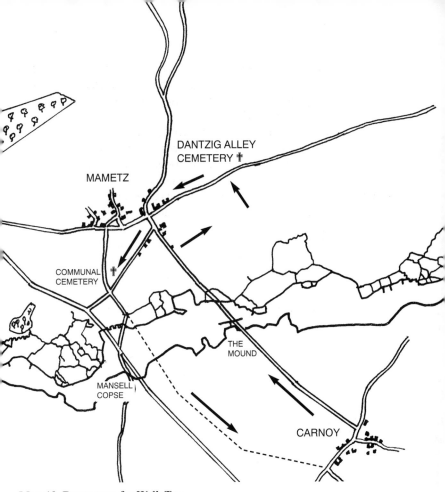

Map 19. Route map for Walk Two.
Boisselle and north east across Mametz and Mametz Wood.

WALK TWO
Starting at Carnoy, the Mound, Dantzig Alley Cemetery, Mametz and the Shrine

This is one of my favourite walks on the Somme, in part because of its links with Manchester's Pals battalions. The initial part of the walk is uphill but it ends with a gentle stroll back towards Carnoy from the north-west. Set aside roughly two and a half hours to complete this walk at leisure. A suitable starting point is the village of Carnoy where there are ample opportunities to park a vehicle. On 1st July 1916 this village was within the 18th Division's sphere of operations although the front lines lay further up the spur of higher land which runs north-

This photograph shows the King, together with the Prince of Wales and Generals Congreve and Rawlinson, being guided between two mine craters at Mametz, during their tour of this area on 10th August 1916. From the slope of the ground I imagine this was taken at Danube Trench, in the area between Mansell Copse and Bois Allemand, attacked across by the 2nd Borders on the morning of 1st July 1916.

east from Carnoy towards Montauban, which was within German occupied ground.

Walk through the village until you reach the road junction where the lane towards Mametz leaves on your left. As you enter this lane Carnoy's communal cemetery is on your right hand side. Walk along the lane in the direction of Mametz, ignoring a small track on your right, until you reach a small valley re-entrant which runs away to your right hand side. On the far side of this small valley the lane rises more steeply for a few yards and this spot was known as The Mound. The British front line crossed the road here at The Mound. Bulgar Trench, the German front line, lay a few yards further up the road, crossing in an east-west course at this point. On the morning of 1st July 1916 the 22nd Manchesters were assembled here at The Mound, with the 1st South Staffs on their left. The 22nd Manchesters were the 7th Division's right hand unit. The German front line here was extensively undermined and charges were detonated at 7.28 am at Bulgar Point, some 300 yards west of The Mound, as well as on the right of the 22nd Manchesters' advance where Bulgar Trench and Austrian Trench joined at the 7th Division's junction with the 18th Division's attack frontage.

Looking due north from The Mound you will see the land rising steadily uphill towards the Montauban–Mametz spur. During 1916 the German Army had constructed a very powerful redoubt at the top of that ground overlooking Mametz. That redoubt was known as Pommiers Redoubt. The site of that redoubt lies to the east of our next objective, Dantzig Alley cemetery.

Continue walking in the direction of Mametz. This open ground was crossed by men of the two supporting battalions, the 2nd Queen's and the 21st Manchesters, on the morning of 1st July 1916. Ignore the first lane after The Mound which leaves on your right in the direction of Montauban. However, in a further 300 metres you will come to a track on the right which again runs in a north-easterly direction. Follow this track which in 1916 was very close to the site of Bulgar Alley trench. Walk up the slope of the Montauban–Mametz spur for roughly 800 metres when you will reach another track. This is the site of Bucket Trench which was captured by the 22nd Manchesters at 7.55 am. Turn left and follow the track along until you reach the Montauban –Mametz road, the D64. Immediately opposite you is Dantzig Alley cemetery with its fine views to the north across the Willow Stream valley towards Bottom Wood, Queen's Nullah, Mametz Wood and Contalmaison.

Walk westwards into Mametz village where you will see the communal memorial as well as one raised recently to the memory of the Manchester Pals and the other units of the 7th Division who attacked Mametz on the morning of 1st July 1916. In the years between the two world wars there was a 7th Division memorial on this site. The capture of Mametz on 1st July 1916 is particularly associated with the 1st South Staffs. Turn left, back onto the Mametz–Carnoy lane, and then immediately right down the lane which leads to the communal cemetery. Looking south, across the valley, you will be able to see Mansell Copse from where the 9th and 8th Devons attacked on 1st July. As you approach the cemetery you will come to where the lane was crossed by Cemetery Trench. On the south-east side of the lane Shrine Alley ran down into the valley where it crossed the Albert - Peronne road at The Halt. Mametz communal cemetery was the site of The Shrine and the machine-gun which Captain Martin of the 9th Devons predicted would cause carnage amongst his men. From here you can see what a clear and uninterrupted view those machine-gunners had across their own front line trench, Mametz Trench,

MANSELL COPSE   MAMETZ

DIRECTION OF
GORDONS' AT

The view towards Mametz from the fields adjacent to Mansell Copse into which the path leading to the Devons cemetery runs on the left of the photograph. The Shrine, within the Communal Cemetery south of Mametz, is centrally located in this photograph. The valley below Mansell Copse was the scene of the attacks by the Gordons on 1st July.

towards Mansell Copse and the Devons' men.

Turn left at the communal cemetery and then keep to the left when the track forks a few yards further on. Follow the track along the valley, parallel to the Albert–Peronne road. This valley is where Sassoon and his battalion were so delayed during the afternoon and evening of 3/4th July and where he saw, 'about 50 of the British dead. Many of them were Gordon Highlanders. There were Devons and South Staffordshires among them, but they were beyond regimental rivalry now...' The Gordons cemetery lies to your right hand side as you walk back towards Carnoy. As you approach the village the Wood on your left is that which was known as Caftet Wood, marked as Bois Caffet on your IGN map. South-west of Caftet Wood, astride the road, was Minden Post at which Malins filmed during 1st July.

WALK THREE
Fricourt village, Shelter Wood, Bottom Wood, the Willow Stream and return

In pre-war years, by comparison with other Somme villages, Fricourt was both large and relatively prosperous. The village was, and is, a warren of small streets with many embankments and cellars suitable for tunnelling under and reinforcing. The German army had come to regard this position as near impregnable and the dug-outs and

152

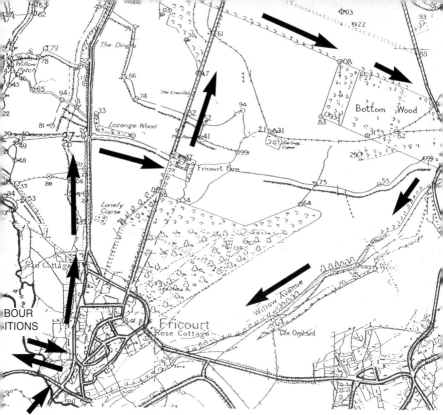

Map 20. Route map for Walk Three.

shell proof protection were indeed very impressive to the British troops which entered the village on 2nd July. To the north east of the village stood Fricourt Wood, and this has changed very little from its pre 1914 shape and size.

I suggest that you begin this walk from the communal cemetery at the D938 / D147 cross-roads south of the village. The British front line was a few yards to the north-east of the cross-roads, running diagonally north-west to south-east. That section which runs towards the south-east was that allotted to the 20th Manchesters for their part of the Subsidiary attack which took place at 2.30 pm on 1st July. Just a short distance to the south-west of the cemetery is Siegfried Sassoon's vantage point (just south of the site of the defunct brickworks *'Ancene Briquie'* on your IGN map) from which position he viewed the initial hours of the Battle of the Somme. Walk towards the village of Fricourt across the course of the Willow Stream. In summer the stream bed is often dry, given the chalk sub strata. The British Military cemetery (Bray Road) lies within No Man's Land and the northern wall of the cemetery lies adjacent to where the German front line crossed the road. This location was known as Wicket Corner. The whole length of front line between the communal cemetery and the Tambour mines was allotted to the 7th Green Howards during the Subsidiary Attack on the village. (See map page 67)

Walk towards the village where you will come to the junction of five lanes. Go straight across, keeping to the D147 in the direction of Contalmaison. One hundred and fifty metres north of the five lane junction you can make a detour to visit the site of the Tambour mine craters if you wish. To reach the craters turn left along the track and the craters can be reached in 300 metres, to the right side of the track. This track marks the northern limits of the attack undertaken by the 7th Green Howards. At the site of the craters the width of No Man's Land was minimal. Here the British Tambour (a pronounced salient) was as close to their German counterparts as were the lines at the Glory Hole, just outside La Boisselle. Apart from the main craters there are still remnants of the minor craters which had been fashioned by the deadly work of the miners in this area during the months leading up to July 1916.

Return to the main street and walk northwards and out of the village in the direction of the German Military cemetery. On your left you will have passed the lane which leads westwards towards the site of the New Military cemetery and just before the German cemetery you will pass a small stand of trees known as Lonely Copse. If you stand on the bank near to the entrance to the German cemetery you will have a panorama of the area attacked by the 8th Somerset Light Infantry due west, the 4th Middlesex and the 10th West Yorks to the south-west at 7.30 am on 1st July. From the rear perimeter of the cemetery you can look out towards Fricourt Wood, nearby to the south-east. To the north-east lies Fricourt Farm which was the first objective of the 21st Division's men on 1st July 1916.

The farm is our own next destination. This can be reached by walking a little way north of the German cemetery and taking a right turn towards the farm. The trees on your left here are those of Lozenge Wood and this marked the furthest advance of the 21st Division's men during the fighting on 1st July. This might be an appropriate moment to remind yourself of Chapter 3's section detailing '2nd July at Fricourt and Mametz'. At the farm turn left. It is worth noting that the site of the farm has been changed from its pre 1914 location and splendour. Prior to the war the farm buildings were located south-east of their present situation. Having turned left at the farm, walk north towards the wood which lies 400 metres distant. One hundred yards north of the farm was a prominent stand of trees known as The Poodles. These have completely disappeared today. Just north of The Poodles the important Crucifix Trench ran north-westwards in the direction of Round Wood and Scots Redoubt. Continue walking towards the trees which form Shelter Wood (Bois de Fricourt Ouest on your IGN map). This location resisted all British attempts to capture it during the early afternoon of 1st July.

As you reach Shelter Wood the track turns right, eastwards. Follow this track and then the right fork which runs down the slope towards a thin finger of woodland. As you descend the slope the oblong shape of Bottom Wood is visible to the east. It is worth noting that before the war Bottom Wood was larger than its present size, extending all the way across to the Mametz–Contalmaison road. Approaching that finger of woodland you will notice that it has been enlarged from its pre-war size. However part of the narrow finger is still discernible as Railway Copse, just south of which an important German trench known as Railway Alley ran from Fricourt Farm eastwards to Bottom Wood. Follow the track along the northern edge of this finger of woodland. This track peters out into a path which leads through the trees in an easterly direction until you come out onto the road between Mametz and Contalmaison. Your understanding of this area might be helped by re-reading Chapter 3's section detailing 'The 4th - 10th July, the fighting for the approaches to Mametz Wood'. The area north of Bottom Wood was the scene of intense fighting involving the 17th (Northern) Division. Looking up the road towards Contalmaison you can see Quadrangle Wood, the small stand of trees on the right of the road 300 metres north of Bottom Wood, just north of which were Quadrangle Trench and Wood Trench.

Walk south towards Mametz. You are now back within the confines of the Willow Stream's valley. Before the war a lane followed the course of the valley and stream in the direction of Fricourt. I propose that you follow the course of that lane by turning right onto the path which runs down the valley (marked as Vallee de Mametz on your IGN map) heading in a south-westerly direction to join the Mametz - Fricourt road. On the opposite side of the road to where the path leaves the Contalmaison road lies Queen's Nullah where Major General Ingouville-Williams was killed whilst commanding the 34th Division. During the bloody month of July 1916, Ingouville-Williams became the most senior of the Army's Somme casualties when he was killed at 7.00 pm on 22nd July. The 34th Division's Diary records the location as being at X.30.a.3,7 on the top of the bank of Queen's Nullah.

Moments earlier Ingouville-Williams had been walking back from a reconnaissance near to Contalmaison, round the south side of Mametz Wood, to meet his car which was waiting on the road towards Montauban. The Major General was killed by the explosion of a chance shell. [2]

Follow the path and valley south-westwards until you reach the Mametz–Fricourt road 200 metres east of Fricourt. Enter the village, keeping to the left at the first junction. This lane will take you back to the five lane junction from where it is a short walk back to the communal cemetery.

WALK FOUR
The Willow Patch, Scots Redoubt and Round Wood from Fricourt

This walk is replicated within the guide to La Boisselle since its vantage points cast illumination upon the areas covered by both guides. That situation reveals the tactical advantage which control of the Fricourt conferred upon whoever controlled this high ground. Your walk here will require the use of the blue series IGN sheet 2408 est (Bray-sur-Somme), although many of the views and points of interest which can be seen from these vantage points are contained within the area covered by 2408 ouest.

The fighting which took place here on 1st July was on the right hand side of the 21st Division's attack. A suitable start can be made from the lane which leaves the D147 Fricourt to Contalmaison road, signposted in the direction of Fricourt New Military Cemetery. After 250 metres you should take the right fork and follow the lane as it rises towards the higher ground. This spur of higher ground lies to the south-east of Sausage Valley and due north of the Tambour mine craters. The German Army had made extensive use of the spur's topography to create a very strong defensive position. On the highest ground was Scots Redoubt, some 400 metres north-west of Round Wood and a little way within the 34th Division's sphere of operations. Its trench map reference was X.21.central. On the western side of the spur lay the Heligoland (Sausage Redoubt) positions, some 500 metres west of Scots Redoubt. Heligoland dominated the wide expanse of No Man's Land across Sausage Valley towards Schwaben Hohe (Lochnagar crater). A little lower on the Fricourt spur was the Willow Patch, marked Bois de Becordel on your IGN map. The Willow Patch lay within the path of the men belonging to 64 Brigade who crossed the German front line known as South Sausage Trench as they fought their

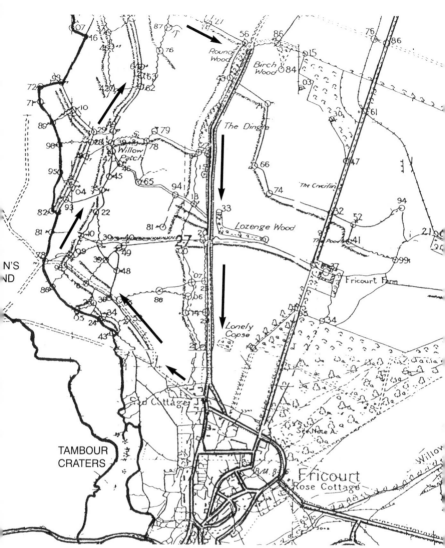

TAMBOUR
CRATERS

Map 21. Route map for Walk Four. (See also page 51)

way up the spur.

In order to reach the Willow Patch and Scots Redoubt continue walking along the lane from Fricourt until you reach the point where the lane breasts the higher ground, from where La Boisselle is visible, roughly 700 metres from the starting point. Here turn right and continue up the spur's slope along a track which runs in the direction of the small woodland which you can see ahead. This is the Willow Patch.

Continue along the track up the spur for a further 600 metres past the Willow Patch. Half way between the Willow Patch and the site of Scots Redoubt lay the boundary between the 21st and 34th Division's spheres of action. Scots Redoubt was a truly commanding position, overlooking both the German occupied villages of Fricourt and La Boisselle, as well as the British held village of Becourt to the south-west. On the morning of 1st July the redoubt here was the scene of intense fighting as men of both 101 and 103 Brigades sought to wrest control from its defenders. To the north other small bands of men belonging to the 24th and 27th Northumberland Fusiliers advanced in ever dwindling numbers towards Contalmaison. Indeed, at times the redoubt was all but surrounded yet still held firm. This is a fine location to stay a while in order to contemplate the complexity of the battlefields visible from this position.

In order to complete the walk continue north-east for a little distance until the track turns sharp right to join the Contalmaison - Fricourt road. Turn right onto that road and walk back towards Fricourt along the sunken lane. The first trees you come to on your right are Round Wood, from where Scots Redoubt lies 400 metres to the north-west. As you return to Fricourt the German Military Cemetery can be seen to your left.

WALK FIVE
Becordel-Becourt, Norfolk Cemetery, the Fricourt spur, Fricourt New Military Cemetery, Fricourt British Cemetery (Bray Road) and return

This walk can be accomplished within three hours. The bulk of the mileage lies in No Man's Land or behind the British lines which existed to the west of Fricourt prior to the First Battle of the Somme, with the exception of that part of Fricourt village which was attacked by various Yorkshire battalions during the first few hours of that battle. You might also like to refer to the section entitled '63 Brigade and the 10th West Yorks' in Chapter 2.

Start from the village of Becordel-Becourt where there is ample parking space near to the communal and military cemeteries. Walk north-eastwards and take the underpass which crosses beneath the D938. This road will take you in the direction of Becourt village and you will see the trees of Becourt Wood ahead on your left. On the right hand side of the road the fields slope up eastwards towards the higher ground of the Fricourt spur. At the top of the visible part of that slope

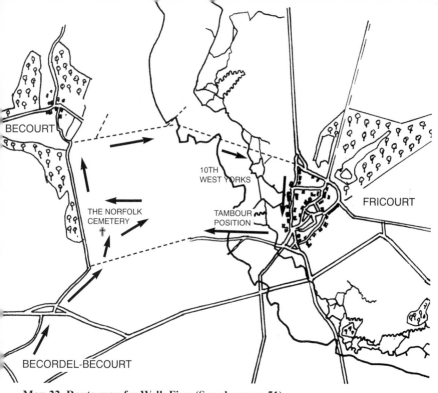

Map 22. Route map for Walk Five. (See also page 51)

Within the map: BECOURT, 10TH WEST YORKS, FRICOURT, THE NORFOLK CEMETERY, TAMBOUR POSITION, BECORDEL-BECOURT

lay Queen's Redoubt where the 10th Yorks (Green Howards) spent part of the night of 30th June 1916. If you wish to visit the site of Queen's Redoubt, from the east of which a good perspective of the Tambour positions west of Fricourt can be had, take the right turn at the cross-roads, 300 metres after the underpass. Walk on for a little over 200 metres and then turn left where a farm track runs uphill above the Norfolk cemetery. After 500 metres you will be at the site of Queen's Redoubt which was on the left side of the track. Walking due east from here will bring you to the Tambour positions. However, if you do not detour towards the Tambour then walk on from the site of Queen's Redoubt until the track peters out whence a footpath will take you back down into the valley, through the new woodland above the Norfolk cemetery.

The Norfolk cemetery contains many noteworthy graves, including that of Major Stewart Walter Loudoun-Shand VC. If you have not already done so, now is the time to visit that cemetery. Continue in the direction of Becourt until, at a bend in the road, you meet a track on the right hand side running up towards the Fricourt spur. This point marked the junction between the spheres of operations of the 21st

Division and the 34th Division to the north. Take this track and walk uphill, ignoring the track which leads off on your left after 200 metres. Continue uphill for a further 500 metres until you reach another fork in the track.

This fork marks the British front line north-west of Fricourt. The battalion which attacked from this position on the morning of 1st July was the 4th Middlesex, with the 10th West Yorks some 300 metres to the south-east and just north of the Tambour positions. No Man's Land was approximately 300 metres wide at this point and the German front line could be found, if you wished to do so, at the end of the track which leads away from the left of your present position. This is the No Man's Land and spur across which Siegfried Sassoon saw soldiers moving from his vantage point in Kingston Road Trench, which was adjacent to Fricourt's communal cemetery to the south. In his book, *Memoirs of an Infantry Officer*, he described the scene.

'I can see the 21st Division advancing about three quarters of a mile away on the left and a few Germans coming to meet them, apparently surrendering. Our men in small parties (not extended in line) go steadily on to the German front line. Brilliant sunshine and a haze of smoke drifting along the landscape. Some Yorkshires a little way below on the left, watching the show and cheering as if at a football match.....'

The 10th Yorks that Sassoon saw and heard cheering 'as if at a football match' were waiting in Queen's Redoubt. Amongst those men was Major Loudoun-Shand, who was destined to lose his life that morning in the act of winning his Victoria Cross.

Otherwise keep straight on, heading eastwards, and now beginning to move downhill across the No Man's Land of spring and early summer 1916. On your right hand side a small grassy path leads down to Fricourt New Military Cemetery and now is the time to visit that place if you have not already done so. That cemetery clearly identifies the area across which the 10th West Yorks attacked on the morning of 1st July. As you continue along the lane in the direction of Fricourt the German front line attacked by the 10th West Yorks, known as Konig Trench, crossed the lane due north of the Tambour mine craters. If you wish to visit the site of these craters access is gained from Fricourt village. Join the lane which now runs down into Fricourt. The houses on your right hand side mark the site of Red Cottage. Turn right onto the D147, the Bray Road, and walk southwards for almost 500 metres when a small track on your right leads off between agricultural buildings. If you wish to make a detour to visit the Tambour mine craters they can be reached after 300 metres along this track. Otherwise continue south until you reach the site of Fricourt British Cemetery (Bray Road). This cemetery is particularly associated with the 7th Yorks (Green Howards) and now is the time to visit this cemetery if you have not already done so.

In order to return to Becordel walk back a few yards in the direction of Fricourt and take the first road on your left. This is the site of Wicket Corner and the German front line wriggled its way northwards from here towards the Tambour positions. South of Wicket Corner, down to the Peronne Road, the German front line was known as Fricourt Trench and that whole length of trench as well as the section north of Wicket Corner up the Tambour was attacked by the 7th Yorks during the Subsidiary Attack at 2.30 pm on 1st July 1916. The front lines from which the 7th Yorks attacked lay some 350 yards to the west of Wicket Corner. Continue to walk westwards for some one and a half kilometres from Fricourt until you reach the Becordel - Becourt road. Turn left onto that road and then pass through the underpass from where you will soon find Dartmoor Cemetery on your right hand side on the road leading into the centre of the village.

THE 1918 TOUR

Map 23. Route map for the 1918 tour.

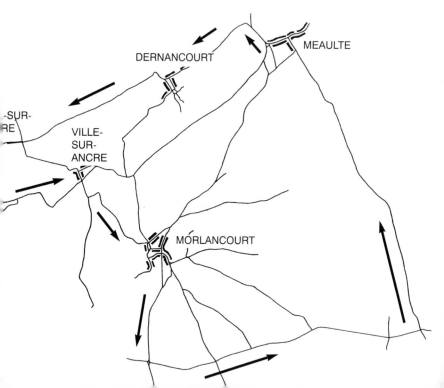

This tour is far too long to consider as a walk. However, it would be an ideal ride for those of you with cycles or as a brief introduction by car to the 1918 fighting. The tour takes in the villages of Buire-sur-l'Ancre, Treux, Ville-sur-Ancre, Morlancourt, Meaulte and Dernancourt in so far as they were affected by the fighting during the last year of the war. This is an ideal route for those of you looking to take in some of the outlying cemeteries to the south-west of the main focus of this guide at Fricourt and Mametz villages. Both the General Tour, which began this chapter, and the first section of Chapter 3 give plenty of detail relating to a number of these more peripheral village's roles in the supply, medical evacuation and billeting of British troops during the 1915 - 16 period. I also suggest that you consult the appropriate cemetery entries at each relevant point.

Start at the village of Buire-sur-l'Ancre on the D52. From here head south to cross the River Ancre in the direction of Treux village. Treux is quite an attractive location. There is a campsite here which provides well sheltered accommodation under mature trees. Having crossed the River Ancre turn left and then follow the D120 past the Ville-sur-Ancre communal and military extension cemeteries on your right until you reach the Ville-sur-Ancre cross-roads. The shortest route to Morlancourt from here is rather rough, impassable by car in winter, but has the merit of leading you to the Morlancourt cemeteries directly. From the Ville-sur-Ancre cross-roads head south and then take the first left, heading up the sunken lane, in the direction of Morlancourt. The exposed and rutted track eventually leads downhill towards the Morlancourt British Number 2 cemetery, within which most of the graves date from 1918. An alternative route is to continue eastwards from Ville-sur-Ancre along the D120 until the signpost on your right directs you towards Morlancourt which you will reach on a more substantial road which is easily passable all year round and leads to the village's communal cemetery. If you wish to visit the two Morlancourt military cemeteries turn right at the communal cemetery and they will soon come into view.

During the German army's spring offensive in 1918 the British were pushed back from their positions outside St. Quentin until they were able to hold a new line just to the east of Ville-sur-Ancre, having lost Albert and the important railway facilities at Dernancourt, Meaulte and Vivier Mill. During that spring offensive the German advance in this area was approximately 30 miles. At this stage the village of Dernancourt lay in No Man's Land whilst Meaulte and Morlancourt were well inside German control. The villages of Buire-sur-l'Ancre

Tanks, photographed during 1918 in the vicinity of Grove Town on the plateau between Meaulte and Happy Valley. [Bob Grundy].

and Treux were therefore just behind the British front lines. During the rest of the summer the position here remained static until, at 4.20 am on 8th August 1918, a massive assault on the German positions east of Amiens was led by the Australian and Canadian Corps under the command of Fourth Army. This assault focused on passing east, towards Foucaucourt and south-east towards Roye. This was the 'Black Day' for the German Army and presaged the last hundred days of more fluid and mobile warfare which led to the collapse of the German Army by late October 1918. Ville-sur-Ancre lay on the northernmost edge of the expected advance and on that day some ground was gained towards Morlancourt until the British troops were positioned on the western outskirts of that village. The following day, 9th August, Morlancourt and Dernancourt villages both fell to the British Army.

Enter Morlancourt village and turn right onto the D42 in the direction of Sailly Laurette. This village of Sailly-Laurette also fell to the British on 8th August 1918. After 2 kilometres along the D42 turn left onto the D1 in the direction of Bray-sur-Somme. By the early morning of 11th August troops belonging to the 4th Australian Division were past Etinehem and in positions west of Bray-sur-Somme and south of Happy Valley. At this stage in the fighting the town of Albert was still in German hands. These positions then remained static for a further ten days time.

On 21st August III Corps the struggle for Albert began, and on the following day the fighting moved across the ridge of high ground east of Morlancourt running between the River Somme, to the south, and the River Ancre to the north-west. The bulk of this was undertaken by the 12th Division, on the northern side of this ridge whilst the 47th

(2nd London) Division fought its way towards Happy Valley. From the cross roads area, north of Etinehem, you will have a fine perspective on those events as well as southwards across the terrain controlled by the 3rd Australian Division on the right of the 47th Division's advance that day. If you wish it is a short detour into Bray thence north to the sites of Bray Vale and Bray Hill cemeteries which contain the graves of many men killed during the fighting for this ridge during the period 22nd to the 26th August 1918.

However, assuming that you have not made the detour, at the cross-roads north of Etinehem just past the Bois des Tailles, near to the French National Cemetery, turn left along the C2. Travel north until the road forks where you should take the left fork. After travelling 1.4 kilometres a right turn would take you across to Grove Town cemetery which contains a small number of 1918 burials. However, there is no necessity to visit Grove Town on this tour, therefore go straight ahead in the direction of Meaulte on the outskirts of which you will find Meaulte Military cemetery with its many graves from 1918's fighting. As we have already seen, the British Fourth Army drew breath in its positions overlooking Bray-sur-Somme on 11th August 1918. On the morning of 22nd August Bray and Meaulte as well as Albert were therefore still in German hands. However, that morning of 22nd August 1918 saw a renewal of Fourth Army's assault which resulted in the re-capture of Albert and Meaulte. That evening British troops were poised above, just to the west, of Happy Valley. Within a short space of time, on the 24th August 1918, Bray-sur-Somme was captured. During the subsequent three days the villages of Fricourt and Mametz were also re-captured by the British and by the 27th August the bulk of the 1916 Somme battlefield had fallen back into British control.

Now enter Meaulte village main street and turn left. Meaulte was lost on 26th March 1918 when the village was evacuated after a rearguard fight involving the 9th (Scottish) Division. It was re-captured on 22nd August 1918 by soldiers from the 12th (Eastern) Division on the opening day of III Corps' attacks as part of the Battle of Albert. At the western end of the main street turn right. After 400 metres take the left fork along the D64 road towards Dernancourt. From Dernancourt return to Buire-sur-l'Ancre along the D52 road.

1. Chalk quarrying and ploughing are rapidly obliterating any visible remnants of the site of Queen's Nullah.

2. Ingouville-Williams' body was recovered and brought back to Warloy-Baillon where he was buried.

Top. Dernancourt Extension.
Centre. Morlancourt. No.2.
Bottom. Gordons Cemetery.

INDEX

167